A Publication of the Ames Foundation

LAMBARDE'S ARCHEION

THE AMES FOUNDATION WAS FOUNDED IN 1910 BY CONTRIBUTIONS OF THE FRIENDS OF JAMES BARR AMES FOR THE PURPOSE OF CONTINUING THE ADVANCEMENT OF LEGAL KNOWLEDGE AND AIDING THE IMPROVEMENT OF THE LAW

ARCHEION

or, a Discourse upon the High Courts of Justice in England

by

William Lambarde

EDITED BY
Charles H. McIlwain
and
Paul L. Ward

HARVARD UNIVERSITY PRESS
CAMBRIDGE, MASSACHUSETTS
1957

Distributed in Great Britain by
Oxford University Press, London

Library of Congress Catalog Card Number: 56-13288

Printed in the United States of America

CONTENTS

INTRODUCTION

Of the contemporary descriptions of the legal and political institutions of England in the later years of Elizabeth's reign, probably the most important are those of Camden, Harrison, Sir Thomas Smith, and William Lambarde. But Camden and Harrison were not lawyers, and Smith, from his training as a civilian, must have been less familiar with the history and working of the courts of common law than Lambarde, who had long been a member of Lincoln's Inn and an Associate of its Bench for some twelve years, before he sent the manuscript of his *Archeion* to Sir Robert Cecil in 1591, upon which the printed editions of 1635 are based. As a common lawyer he was in constant contact with others of the same profession, and must have known of their growing hostility to the Courts of Equity, of Requests, of Star Chamber, and of High Commission. But in his later life he was also the friend of Sir Thomas Egerton and of Sir Julius Caesar, and when the latter wrote to Lord Burleigh in defence of the Court of Requests in 1597/8 he suggested that "if your Lo^{p} being continewally imployed in ye great affaires of this state, shall finde no leisure to read ouer matters of this nature; then it maie please your Lo^{p} that Mr William Lamberd, whoe is A gentleman of great learning & sincerity, or some other one or more of like sufficiency might be intreated to peruse suche Collections as I haue gathered . . . And theruppon to make report of so muche as he or they shall finde proued, that her Ma^{tees} Court of

Whitehall, maie enioye suche authoritie as to the same of right belongeth."

It is no doubt true, as Thomas Fuller says, that Lambarde's "labours are feasts for scholars, not (like Stow's works) daily fare for common people," and this may account for the fact that while the important works of Smith and Harrison and Camden are available everywhere in modern editions, the *Archeion* has never been reprinted since its first appearances in 1635.

It was this that led Professor Ward and me to think that a new edition might now be worth while, not alone because of Lambarde's profound knowledge of the history and the procedure of the courts, but also because his account was written at a critical period in the development of the English constitution and is thus an exceptionally impartial indication of contemporary opinion concerning courts and procedures that by 1641 had come to be considered "an intolerable burden to the subjects, and the means to introduce an arbitrary power and government."

In Lambarde's "Epistle Dedicatorie" addressed to Sir Robert Cecil he says that some parts of the *Archeion* were "penned sundrie yeeres sithence, others not long agoe, and the rest so lately, that your Honour may, if it please you, take the first view and reading of them." Many of these earlier drafts of the *Archeion* are now in public libraries, and microfilms of some of the most important have been obtained, which often indicate significant changes over the years in the author's views, and changes that he probably shared with many of his contemporaries. This, if nothing else, makes the contents of these early drafts a subject of the greatest importance in the constitutional and intellectual history of England.

In one of them there is interesting indication that some parts of Sir Thomas Smith's *De Republica Anglorum* may in its earlier form be copied from one of Lambarde's early drafts.

These matters, and all others connected with the earlier versions of the *Archeion*, it seemed better to reserve for separate treatment instead of placing them in the footnotes in this edition. The appendix, which examines the relation of the two editions of 1635 to what Lambarde himself wrote in 1591 and thereafter, is the work of Professor Ward alone.

C. H. McIlwain

ACKNOWLEDGMENTS

We wish to express appreciation for the courtesies and assistance unfailingly provided by the staffs of the Harvard Law Library, the Houghton Library, and the Folger Shakespeare Library—in particular by Miss Eleanor Little in the Treasure Room of the first of these, during the weeks of collating. The Society of Fellows of Harvard University generously provided financial help for the initial copying of the text. We are grateful to the authorities of the British Museum and Bodleian Library for microfilms consulted, to the Ames Foundation for help that made this publication possible, and to the officials of the Harvard University Press for their understanding and skill in handling the details of publication.

C. H. M.
P. L. W.

LAMBARDE'S ARCHEION

The reader who chooses to read the following closely may appreciate a preliminary word of explanation. This, the standard edition of the *Archeion*, was plainly issued by the author's heir, T. L., in indignant correction of errors made in the "untimely publication" of the same book a few months earlier. Since the accuracy of T. L.'s corrected edition is itself open to some questions, we have felt it advisable to supply in footnotes the variant readings from several sources:

F, the unauthorized earlier publication, ascribable to a printer named Frere;

H, Harvard Law MS. 68, a copy of the *Archeion* that seems datable around 1600; and

BT and *WF*, manuscripts written before 1590 (one now in the Bodleian Tanner collection and the other at Washington in the Folger Library) that are authoritative copies of the separate commentaries which Lambarde drew together in 1591.

The significance of the variant readings is explored at length in the appendix.

[*A 1]

ARCHEION,[1]

OR,

A DISCOURSE[2]

Upon the High Courts OF IUSTICE *IN* ENGLAND.

Composed[3] by *William Lambard*, of *Lincolnes Inne*, Gent.

Newly[4] Corrected, and enlarged according to the *Authors* Copie.

Omnia judicia, aut detrahendarum controversiarum: aut puniendorum maleficiorum causa reperta sunt, Cic.[4]

LONDON,
Printed by *E. P.*[5] for *Henry Seile*, dwelling at the Tygers-head in St. *Pauls Church-yard.*[5] 1635.

---

[1] Archeion] Archion *F (the edition printed by Frere earlier in 1635).*
[2] Discourse] Comentary *F.*
[3] Composed] Compiled *F.*
[4] Newly . . . sunt, Cic.] *om. F.*
[5] by E. P. . . . Church-yard] for Daniel Frere, and are to be sold at his shop in little Brittaine, at the signe of the Red Bull *F.*

[*A 3]

The AUTHORS Epistle.

Dedicated[6] to the Right Honorable Sir *Robert Cecil*, Knight, one of her Majesties *most Honourable Privie* Councell.

ALBEIT, right Honorable Sir; that my bounden Dutie towards you, aswell for the singular favour of my most Honorable Lord your Father, continually [*A 3v] *extended upon me, as also for that* cheerefull Regard *which it hath pleased your Selfe to vouchsafe unto me, might have moved me with the first, to gratulate unto You, that Honourable place wherunto you are right worthily advanced: Yet that I may not onely bewray my ioy thereof in vanishing words, but testifie it also with some more standing* Memoriall *that might remain: I have purposely spared to see your Honour, untill that* [*A 4] *I might come accompanied with this Copie of mine* Archeion,[7] *or* Commentaries of the Courts of England; *Whereof, some I penned sundrie yeeres sithence, others not long agoe, and the rest so lately, that your Honour may, if it please you, take the first view and reading of*

---

[6] The Authors Epistle. Dedicated] The Epistle As it was Dedicated in the Manuscript, *F.*

[7] Archeion] Archion *F.*

them; wherein[8] *if you shall finde either pleasure or profit, then shall I also both enioy the desire of my heart, and the expected fruit of my Travaile. And thus heartily* [*A 4v] *praying* God *to increase your Honor with your yeers, that as you bee already by Nature the Sonne; so you may at the length by imitation become the very* Heire *of that renowned* Nestor, *and onely* Atlas *of the* English *Countrie and Commonwealth. I humbly pray you to pardon the escapes both of me and this Writer. From* Lincolnes Inne *this* 22. *of* October, 1591.

Your Honors to command,[9]
Wil. Lambard.

---

[8] wherein] where *F.*
[9] to command] at commandment *F.*

[*A 5]

To the Reader.[10]

Corruptio unius est generatio alterius.

FOR had not this late *aspersion* trenched too much upon the *pietie* I owe to so worthie an *Ancestor* (as I dare say) the *Kingdome* would acknowledge; truly I should not have given my least *assent* to have advanced this to light, [*A 5v] (which too lately was, without my privitie, or liking.) But the crying *Errors* (arising from the *untimely publication*) call upon me, to *vindicate* him from that *wrong* (if any such can be) and my selfe from an imputed *Apathie*. But why doe I call them *wrongs*, and *aspersions?* since that sweet *Odour* hee hath left, cannot by their false *ingredients* be so *sophisticated*, but may by the *judicious* bee easily smelt out. And for those that delight meerely in *superficials*, neither weighing the *sense*, or *defects*, but swallow the *Errours* for *Errataes;* such as these it hath [*A 6] alreadie passed. Others are to be expected, of meere *active soules;* and of these, some that will passe *sentence* (upon the Booke) before it come to *judgement:* I shall *assigne* them the *Character*, heeretofore occasioned upon this verie *Worke;*

Fooles will contend,
without the cause discerning,
And argue most,
of what they have no learning.

I have too much digressed: seeing my *desires* are to be *repaired*, for *injuries* past; not to labour to prevent I know [*A 6v] not what, to come: Grant me the *first*, and I shall *appeale* the *other* to thy *judgement;* and thinke, I have well tendred my *dutie* I owe to my *Parents*, and *Countrey*.

T. L.

---

[10] *This editorial preface replaces the following in F:* To the Ingenious Reader. Next the Knowledge of GOD, and our selves, that of our Country takes place, as most usefull and necessary . . . fortunate is he, who dying can say to the Common-wealth wherein hee liv'd, I have made thy good, and preservation my only care. Which granted, I dare be bold to pronounce the Author of this Booke very happy . . . The dignity of the Treatise it selfe, refuseth my Approbation as needlesse . . . I dare promise it long life . . . Farewell.

[*A 7]

The Contents.[11]

[References are to the pages of the original edition.]

---

[11] *The following table does not appear in F or in any MS consulted. The various indentations are the present editor's.*

[12] *This and the preceding entry refer only to explanatory notes in the margin of the text.*

[*A 8]

---

[13] *Refers to a marginal heading marking what is only a passing mention in the text.*

[14] *Refers to a marginal heading for the second half of a long paragraph; notice that here it is out of page order.*

ARCHEION,

OR,

The High Courts of *Iustice* in England.

Contention hath beene from the beginning.

AS there is no doubt, but that continually, even from the first propagation of Mankinde upon the Face of the Earth, there hath been before the Floud, *Cain*, *Cainists*, and proud *Gyants*; and after the Floud, *Cham*, *Nimrod*, *Esau*, and such others; migh-

Facsimile of page 1 of Thomas Lambarde's edition

[*1]

ARCHEION,[15]

OR,

The[16] High Courts of *Iustice* in *England*.

CONTENTION HATH BEENE FROM THE BEGINNING.

AS there is no doubt, but that continually, even from the first propagation of Mankinde upon the Face of the Earth, there hath been before the Floud, *Cain*, *Cainists*, and proud *Gyants*; and after the Floud, *Cham*, *Nimrod*, *Esau*, and such others, mightie [*2] hunters, and injurious oppressors of the servants of God: So it is not to be thought, but from time to time, even sithence also God hath of his fatherly care and mercifull providence, alwayes stirred up some of his owne, whom hee hath endowed and armed with sufficient *Wisdome*, *Authoritie*, and *Power*, not onely to preserve his little ones from the greedie jawes of such ravenous persecutors; but also after some sort to resist their furie, and to chastise them for their excesse and outrage. And hereof it was, that whilest all the world consisted of a few Householders, the Elder (or Father of the Family) exercised authoritie over his

---

[15] Archeion] *H BT;* Archion *F. For a discussion of these texts, see the Appendix, pp. 143–167.*

[16] Or, The] *F;* Or of the *H BT.*

Meyney, and did distribute Reward and Paine amongst them after his owne discretion, according as the old Poet saith,

Iura dant singuli natis & uxoribus.

[*3] THE BEGINNING OF KINGDOMES.

But after such time as by Multiplication of *Families* and *Hamlets*, naturall Love was somewhat more cooled, as being derived, and drawne further from the Fountain: And after such time also, as greedinesse of enjoying the fat of the Land had moved debate and dissention, sometimes from[17] the Limits of grounds (whereof the word *Lis* tooke the name) sometime for the use of a *River* or *Water* that ran betweene the possessions of two men, (whereof also such *Contenders* were called *Rivales*) and sometimes for some other causes; but yet so, that alwayes the mightier, and more mischievous, did (as Bulls in the *Heard*) gore and grieve the weaker and better[18] sort. Then fled men (as *Cicero* conjectureth) to some one [*4] among them, excelling others in *Vertue*, and submitted themselves unto him, praying that hee would by *equity* save them from *injury*, and maintaine both the *mightiest* and the *meanest* in one indifferencie of *right* and *justice*. And truly, so long as they found this at his hand, they tooke for *Law* whatsoever hee pronounced, and they obeyed (as an Oracle) whatsoever was commanded by him.

THE BEGINNING OF LAWES.

But when as (at the length) hee also either did convert to his singular gaine, that Authority which was given unto him for the common benefit of others, or else dealt not a like measure unto all; but abandoning *Iustice*, made *Lust* his *Iudge*, and *Might* his *Minister;* then forthwith alteration of the former

---

[17] from] *F;* for *H BT.*

[18] and better] *H BT; om. F.*

[*5] estate followed, and then were *lawes* and *rules* of *Iustice* devised, within the which (as within certaine *Limits*) the power of *Governors* should from henceforth be bounded, and which should have but one *tongue* and *voyce*, wherewith to speake to all sorts of Suiters. (†)[19]

THE BEGINNING OF COURTS OF IUSTICE.

Againe, after all this also, when not only the multitude of men was growne infinite; but wickednesse also was much increased with the time; and consequently *contentions* waxed so many in number, and manifold in matter, as neither any one person was found able to determine the *Suits*, nor any one place sufficed to containe the *Suitors:* Then accordingly (as *Iethro* advised *Moses*) the *Iurisdiction* (or *chardge* of administring *Iustice*) was first [*6] broken into parts, the *hearing* of *causes* was divided amongst many persons, and sundry *places* were appointed to that speciall end, and service. Whereof it came to passe, that the *Israelites* (which were the first people of the world, to whom any *written Law* was given) did pronounce their *Iudgements* in the Gates of every Citie, to the end, that both all men might behold the indifferencie of their proceedings, and that no man should need to goe out of his way to seeke *Iustice.*

The old *Romans* first within their *Temples*, of purpose to shew that *Iudgement* was a *Divine thing;* then afterward in *Curia & Foro.* The *Athenians* also, and[20] their *Temple* called (by reason of a speciall judgement) *Areopagus*, and in the places called *Palladium* and *Pritaneum:* And albeit that the *Gauls* (our [*7] Neighbours, that bee now called *Frenchmen*)

(†) *Iura inventa metu iniusti, fateare necesse est.* Horat.

---

[19] sorts of Suiters] *H;* sorts of men *F;* men *BT.*

[20] and] *F;* in *H BT.*

did hold their Assemblies for *Iustice* only at *Carnute* or *Chartres*, a place so situate in the middest of their Countrie, that all the people might have indifferent resort thereunto: After which order also the *Britans* of this *Iland* did make their like meetings as it might be well gathered out of *Caesars Commentaries*, where he plainly writeth, that those *Druydes* (which then were the *Iudges* amongst the *Gauls*) had fetched that their manner of *Discipline* out of *Britaine*, where wee now dwell: Yet neverthelesse, the *Saxons*, our Ancestors, (which succeeded them in this Countrie) they (I say) retained the manner of the old *Germans*, their owne Elders, who (as *Tacitus* writeth) *Iura per pagos vicosque reddebant;* and they made distribution of *Iustice*, not onely in one Towne, [*8] or in the Princes *Palace*, but also at sundry other speciall places within the Countrie.

And truly, the *Normans* (that invaded the posteritie of the same *Saxons* here) did not so much alter the substance, as the name of the *Saxons* order, which they found at their comming hither.

Of Courts.[21]

For (in effect) they did but change the word *Gemot*, which in the *Saxon tongue* signified an *Assembly* (or *Meeting*) into the *French* word *Court*, or *Cour;* (for so it is also found written) being a terme of the selfe-same force and signification.

What a Court[22] signifieth.

This *Court*, or *Cour*, therefore is derived of the *Latine Curia;* which also is fetched from *Cura*, (as *Valla* writeth) whereby it is notified, that heed and care ought to be [*9] taken in the deciding of Controversies.

---

21 Of Courts] Gemote *F BT; om. H.*

22 What a Court] Cour what it *F;* Courte what it *H BT*.

It signifieth properly both the Assembly of men for the hearing of Causes in variance, and the place also where the Assembly is made: According to the first of which significations, the *Saxons* (as I said) called it (†)*Gemot*, a *meeting*, of *Gemettan*, to *meet:* and agreeable to the second, the Kings house was first called a *Court*, because the chiefe *Court* of *Iustice* was holden there.

The Division of Courts.

But now of *Courts*, some may be called *Ecclesiasticall*, some, *Lay;* and othersome, mixed, (that is to say) both *Ecclesiasticall* and *Lay*.

Ecclesiasticall[23] Courts, what they be.[23]

Ecclesiasticall Courts be many in number, and divers in nature; [*10] whereof the greatest, is the *Convocation* of all the *Archbishops, Bishops,* and whole Clergy of both the *Provinces* of *Canterburie* and *Yorke;* the which is alwayes summoned by the Kings[24] Writ, and which can doe nothing without the *Royall assent* first had and obtained. (‡)

And[25] *so the spirituall Prelats of the upper House being assembled by the Queenes Writ in the* Convocation, *might after appeale made unto them, determine of matter touching the Queene.*[25]

The next to those, be the two *Provinciall Synodes* of *Canterburie* and *Yorke:* to the latter of the which, there are onely

(†) Which signifieth a meeting (*ad exercitationes Legis congressus*) from whence we have the word *Mootes*.

(‡) 13. *Eliz. cap.* 12. 24. *H.* 8. *cap.* 12.

---

[23] Ecclesiasticall . . . be] Ecclesiasticall Courts *F BT; om. H.*

[24] Kings] *F;* Queenes *H.*

[25] And . . . Queene] *F; om. H BT. Note that Thomas Lambarde shifted this into italics, as if he felt it possibly an insertion.*

three *Bishoprickes* subject; that is to say, *Durham*, *Carlile*, and *Chester:* all the residue owing their *obedience* to the *Sea* of *Canterburie*.

Then follow the Court of the *High Commissioners*,[26] in Causes of *Religion*, [*11] and the *Court* of *Delegates;* to the which there lyeth *Appeale*, from sentence given in the *Arches*.

After these, be the generall *Courts* of the *Archbishop* of *Canterburie;* that is to say, the *Consistorie*, (or *Court* of *Arches*) as well for *Appellations*, as for matters of the first instance.

The *Court* of *Audience*, (or the *Chancelors Court*) which was wont to bee holden in the *Archbishops* House.

The *Commissaries* (or the *Prerogative*) *Court*, for *Probats* of *Testaments;* and the *Court* of *Faculties*, for *Dispensations:* if at the least, that may be called a *Court*, which holdeth no Plea of controversie.

Lastly, the speciall *Courts* of this *Archbishop*, namely, the *Consistorie*, holden by his *Commissarie* at *Canterbury*, for his owne Diocesse; his *Archdeacons Court*, and the *Court* of those peculiar *Deaneries*, which doe [*12] belong to him, and doe lye in the Diocesse of other *Bishops*.

The other *Archbishop* (and each other *Bishop* also) hath in his[27] Diocesse the *Court* of his *Chancelor*, and the *Court* of his *Archdeacon*, or *Officiall*.

But for as much as the description of these *Ecclesiasticall Courts* pertaineth to another Learning, I meane to the *Civill* and *Canon* Lawes (by which they be governed;) and for that they doe not peculiarly (as the rest) belong to our Nation, and may withall require a severall Treatise by themselves; I will at this time content my selfe with this bare enumeration of them, as bending my labour chiefely to the discoverie of

---

[26] the High Commissioners] *H;* High Commission *F.*

[27] his] *F;* his owne *H BT.*

the *Lay* or *Temporall Courts* that had, or now have place amongst us.

[*13] LAY COURTS OF TWO SORTS IN ANCIENT TIME.

Lay Courts were at first of two sorts onely, *Base* and *High:* Concerning the beginning whereof, I read, that even as *Moses* (the speciall Minister of *Iustice* appointed by God, finding himselfe unable to sustaine the burthen of deciding all controversies of the people) did set *Iudges* over *Tribes*, *Hundreths*, *Fifties*, and *Tenths* of the multitude; to whom he referred the determination of smaller causes; reserving to himselfe the knowledge of matters that were of greater importance.

THE FIRST DIVISION OF THIS REALME, FOR IURISDICTION.

So also the *Saxon*, (but Christian King of *England*) *Alfred*, divided [*14] this whole Realme first into *Shires*, then those *Shires* into *Lathes*, *Rapes*, or *Ridings*, and those againe into *Wapentakes*, or *Hundreds;* and lastly, those also into *Leets*, *Boroughs*, or *Tythings:*(†) and did withall establish *Iurisdiction* in every of these, permitting to the *Reeves* (or *Iudges* of the lower Roomes) Authoritie of hearing smaller Suits, granting greater power to the *Sheriffe*, and *Aldermen*, which had charge of greater Assemblies, and retayning to himself the decision of such matters, as by just cause of Appellation, either for *Law*, or *Equitie*, should be brought unto him.

Shire-Mote, or *Shire*-Court.[28]

The Court of the whole *Shire* was of two sorts: whereof the first then called *Scyregemote*, that is, the Assemblie of the

(†) *Ingulf. Croyland*, 12. *H.* 7. 17.*b*. *Fineux.*

---

[28] Shire-Mote, or Shire-Court] *F; om. H;* Scyregemote *BT.*

Shire (and now termed the *Sheriffes-turne*) was then (as now also) holden twice a yeare.

And this *Court* was of like *Iurisdiction* [*15] to the *Court* of the *Leet*, or of the *Burroughs* or *Tythings*, as it was then called.

Hundred Court. Court *Baron*.

The second and the *Hundred Court*, then named *Hundresmote*,[29] was in those dayes appointed to bee holden once in a month at the least, and that was of like nature to the *Countie-Court*, (which is now kept once every moneth also:) And to the Court *Baron*, anciently called *Heal-gemot*, and corruptly *Haylemot*, that is, (as I said) the Court of the *Hall*, *Mannor*, or chiefe place which is now at this day to bee kept, and maintained once in three weekes, if the Lord will so have, and use it.

I read further in the Lawes of the *Saxon* King *Edgar* (†) thus, *Negesecenam man won Cyng rot*[30] *&c.*

> Let no man seeke to the *King* in matter of variance, unlesse he cannot find *right* at home: but if that *right* be too heavie for him, then let [*16] him seeke to the *King*, to have it lightned.

The very like whereof, in effect, is to be seene in the Lawes of *Canutus* the *Dane*, sometime King of this *Realme* also: Out[31] of which Law,[32] I gather foure things.

(†) *Sax. Lawes, Cap.* 2. *f.* 79.

---

[29] Hundresmote] Undnedizemore *F;* hundredesgemote (*in Saxon letters*) *H BT*.

[30] Negesecenam man won Cyng rot] Nazace *F;* Ne gesece nan man thone Cyng (*in Saxon letters*) *H BT*.

[31] *With this word F H BT all start a new paragraph marked with section heading:* The High Court of Justice before the Conquest for Law and Equity (*which our text has instead on p.* *19).

[32] Law] *F;* lawes *H BT*.

1. First, That every man had meanes to sue in those *base Courts* at home in the Countrey, for the recoverie of his right.

2. Then, that no man ought to sue out of the Countrey, or to draw his *Plea* from thence, without good cause; both which things doe lye plainely in the Letter of this *Law*.

3. Thirdly, that the *King* himselfe had a *High Court* of *Iustice*, wherein, it seemeth, that he sate in person: For the words be, *Let him not seeke to the King*.

4. And lastly, that the same *Court* of the *King* did judge not onely according to meere *Right*, and [*17] *Law*, but also after *Equitie* and good *Conscience*.

For first the words be, (*Unlesse he cannot finde right at home:*) by which it is permitted, that then hee might sue to the *King* for *right*. Againe, the words stand thus; *If that Right be too heavie, then let him seeke to the King, &c.* whereby it is meant, that hee should have the *rigour* of the *Law* mitigated by the *conscience* of the *Prince*. And after this order, and in those two sorts of *Courts* was all *Iustice* administred, untill the time of *King William* the *Conquerour:* During whose Reigne (as also under the Government of *King Rufus*, his Sonne) it is to be thought, that the ordinarie course of *Iustice* was greatly disturbed, as well by reason of the intestine and forraine *Warres*, as also because that these two *Princes* governed by a meere and absolute [*18] power, as in a Realme obtained by *Conquest*.

But yet it was so farre off, that any of them did utterly abolish these *Courts*, that the same did not only remaine during all their times (howsoever put to silence for a season;) but also had continuance afterwards, and doe yet (as they may) beare life amongst us.

For (as I said) those *base Courts* of the *Shires*, *Hundreds*, *Burroughes*, and *Mannors*, doe yet remaine (in a manner) the same in substance that they then were. And that the *Pleas* ought no more to be taken from them now in our dayes (without cause) than they ought then to have beene, may evidently be proved by the *Writs* of *Folt*[33] *Pone*, *Accedas ad Curiam*, and *Recordare*, which wee now yet use; and that to this onely end, to remove *Suits* (upon cause) out of one *Court* into another.

[*19] THE KINGS BENCH.[34]

The High Court of *Justice* before the Conquest
for *Law* and *Equity*.

The like I may also affirme of that *High Court*, which then followed the *King* himselfe; and is[35] thereof, till this day, called the *Bench* of the *King*.[35] For albeit that many peculiar *High Courts* be now, sithence that time, advanced, by reason that the multitude of *Suits* still encreasing with the iniquitie and age of the *World*, would not suffer them all to be ordered in one place, without both intollerable delay of matters, and great vexation of men: Yet neverthelesse, if you will throughly behold the matter and subject about which all these *Courts* are now occupied, you shal perceive, that they are but, as it were, so many branches sprung out of that one Tree, or streames derived from the same Spring and Fountaine.

[*20] For letting passe those Courts of the Countrie, which I have already touched; and also those other smal Courts of *Record*, that be in Cities and Townes corporate; yea, and the *Pye-Powders* Court(†) it selfe, that lasteth no longer than the *Faire*; I say, that all our Higher Courts at this day, be

(†) *Pye Powders*, of *Pyes* feet, and *Powlders* dustie, because it is for Travellers to the Faire.

---

[33] Folt] Tolt *F H BT* (*BT reads* Tolt, Pone).

[34] The Kings Bench] *H; om. F BT.*

[35] and is . . . King] *H; om. F BT.*

either Courts of *Rights*[36] and *Law*, or else of *Equitie* and *Conscience*, as they then were; although they now require another subdivision than they then had, and that if you will, may be this.

THE DIVISION OF MEERE[37] LAY COURTS AT THIS DAY.

The Courts of *Law* doe either hold[38] *civill*, or *criminall* Causes (more[39] anciently tearmed *Common Pleas*, and *Pleas* of the *Crowne*)[39] and these *civill* Causes be either moved betweene the *Prince* himselfe, and [*21] his *Tenants* and *Subjects;* or else betweene *Subjects* themselves; and that either of our own *Realme* only, or of it, and another *Realme*.

Those Courts of *Law* that hold *Plea* of *common*, or *civill* matters growing betweene the *King*, or the *Prince*, and his *Subjects*, be these: The *Exchequer*, devised for the safe custodie of the *Crowne-lands*, and for the faithfull answering of the *Revenues* of the same. The Court of *Wards* and *Liveries*, the Court of the *Dutchy* of *Lancaster*, and the *Chancery* Court, at the least so farre forth as the same hath to doe with *Petitions*, *Travers juram.*[40] *de droit*, and such like causes.

Those other Courts of *Law*, that have *Iurisdiction* of *civill* or *common Pleas*, arising betweene our owne *Subjects*, be these:

The *Common Pleas*, or *Bench;* the *Marshalsey*, for matters within [*22] the *Verge*, or limits assigned to the Kings House, or Palace.

The *Admiralty Court* for *marine* causes, and the *Kings Bench*, so farre forth as it doth[41] retaine *jurisdiction* in matters of *Debt*, *Assumption*, *Actions* upon the *case*, and such other

---

36 Rights] *F;* Right *H BT.*
37 meere] *H;* the *F; om. BT.*
38 hold] handle *F H BT.*
39 (more . . . Crowne)] *H; om. F BT.*
40 Travers juram.] *F;* Traversies, monstrans *H BT.*
41 doth] *F;* doth yett *H BT.*

things more properly tryable in the *Common place*, than[42] here;[43] and these be the Courts of meere Law, that have ordinary[44] resort and limited[45] Iurisdiction.

The Courts of absolute[46] *conscience* for *civill* Causes, be these; The *Chancerie* open to all men: The Court of *Requests*, that specially heareth the Suits of poore men, and of the Princes servants.

The *Chancellors* Court within the *Exchequer*, and the two Councells establisht the one in *Wales*, the other in the *North-countrey*, both consisting of *President* and *Counsell*, like unto those which in *France* [*23] are commonly called *Parliaments*.

Criminall Causes belong yet still[47] either generally to the *Kings Bench;* or specially[48] to the Court of *Star-chamber;* or else particularly[49] to the *Constables* Court, to the *Marshalsey*, *Admiraltie*, *Gaol-deliverie*, *Oyer* and *Terminer*,[50] and *Sessions of Peace* for our owne Subjects, or to the *Wardens* Courts in the *Marches*, for causes of that kind between us and the *Scots*.

The order[51] of this discourse of *Lay Courts*.[51]

But now, to the end that it may the more evidently appear, how, and by what degrees of encrease these many Courts have sprung out of that one, it is requisit that I proceed in the History of King *William* the Conqueror, where I left, and descend from him downward, untill I have set them all on foot, some[52] in the order which I have laid, and some Historically, as[53] the time it selfe begat them.

---

[42] more properly tryable in the Commonplace, than] *H;* properly tryable in the Common place and not *F BT*.

[43] here] *F;* there *H BT*.

[44] ordinary] *F BT;* anie ordinary *H*.

[45] limited] *H; om. F BT*.

[46] absolute] *H; om. F BT*.

[47] yet still] *H; om. F BT*.

[48] specially] *H; om. F BT*.

[49] particularly] peculiarly *H;* specially *F BT*.

[50] Terminer] *F;* determyner *H BT*.

[51] The order . . . Courts] *F; om. H BT*.

[52] some] *H;* not *F*.

[53] and some Historically, as] *H;* but Historically, and as *F*.

[*24] THE COURT OF EXCHEQUER.

It is confessed by all Writers,[54] that the *Conquerour* (after such time as he had suppressed the forces of those that made head against him here) did immediately cause the whole *Realme* to be exactly surveyed by *Shires* and *Hundreds* severally; as well for the understanding of Woods, Pastures, Meadowes, and Tillages thereof, as also for the profit[55] of Churches, Mills, Villains, and of all other commodities whatsoever. The Record of which Survey was then called *Doomes-day Book*, and was appointed to be kept in the *Exchequer* at *Westminster;* where it now resteth.

And that *Court* also did he then newly erect for the order of his *Revenues*, after the name of his *Exchequer* in *Normandie*, though in the [*25] manner thereof it differed not a little from it: For the *Exchequer* of *Normandie* had not onely the government of the *Revenues* of the *Duke* there, but was also the Soveraigne *Court* for administration of *Iustice* among his subjects; and so continued, untill that *Lewis* the twelfth, King of *France*, in the yeare after *Christ*, 1499. converted it into a *Court* of *Parliament*, consisting of President and Counsellors, and established it at *Roan* in *Normandie*, where it now remaineth.

But this his *Exchequer* in *England* had onely the direction of his *Demesnes* and *Receipts;* the administration of common *Iustice* continuing still in that other *High Court* of his, as it was before his comming hither.

For proofe of which matter, I call to witnesse *Gervasius Tilburiensis*, a learned man, that lived so neere to [*26] the time of the *Conquest*, that he confessed that he had conference with *Henry* the Bishop of *Winchester*, which was sonne to the *Conquerours* owne Sister.

---

54 Writers] *F; writings H BT.*

55 for the profit] *F;* of the Profitts *H BT.*

This man was an *Officer* of the *Exchequer* here, and penned speciall *Dialogues* of the *Observations* of the *Exchequer*, which hee dedicated to King *Henry* the second, and be yet remaining in the *Receipt*, under the custodie of the *Chamberlaines* of the *Exchequer*, in the *Blacke booke* there. In the first part of which his *Dialogues*, and the first *Chapter*, hee writeth (for[56] the *antiquitie* of the *Exchequer*) that it was brought out of *Normandie* by the *Conquerour;* and for the *authoritie* of that *Court*, hee hath (amongst other words) these following: *Nulli licet Statuta Scaccarii infringere, vel eis quavis temeritate resistere; habet enim hoc commune cum ipsa Domini Regis Curia, in qua* [*27] *ipse in propria persona Iura decernit, quod nec Recordationi nec Sententiae in eo latae liceat alicui contradicere*. Whereby it is plainely proved, that the *Court* of the *Exchequer* was at that time a distinct *Court* from that *Court* of the *King;* in the which he himselfe sometimes, and commonly his *Iustice* (called then *Prima Iustitia*) did use to sit: The one *Court* having authoritie over the Kings *Demeasnes* and *Receipts*, as *Gervasius* (in all that Worke) at large discourseth; and the other using the power of distributing common *Iustice*, as his words in this place, doe sufficiently purport.

And therefore I cannot but (here by the way) note the error of them(†) which doe maintaine, that the *Exchequer* was (in this time of King *Henry* the second) a *Court* of whatsoever *Common Pleas* for all subjects [*28] whatsoever, and which (for proofe of their Assertion) doe alledge the Title of Master *Glanviles* Booke in part thus: *Et illas solum Leges continet, & consuetudines, secundum quas Placitatur in Curia Regis ad Scaccarium.*

For overthrow whereof, first I say, that the words of the Title bee not the words of *Glanvile* himselfe, but of that man

(†) *Commentar. f.* 208. *Sand.*

---

[56] for] for the advancement of *FH BT.*

(whatsoever hee were) that published his Book in *Print;* for hee intituleth his[57] Book thus:

Tractatus de legibus de tempore[58] *Regis Henrici secundi, compositus illustri viro Ranulpho de Glanvillo juris regni, & antiquarum consuetudinum eo tempore peritissimo:* which doth plainly bewray that he spake[59] of *Glanvile* as of another man, and which also lived not then, but at another time.

Secondly, I affirme, that if it were the speech of *Glanvile* himself, [*29] yet if you will take the rest of his words with you, you[60] shall see that they have another meaning: for the words stand together, *Secundum quas placitatur in Curia Regis ad Scaccarium, & coram Iustitiis ubicunq; fuerint:* so that if you read them with the point *Comma* next after the word *Regis*, then they will yeeld you three Courts, that is to say, the *Exchequer*, the Kings Court[61] (or *Bench*) or[62] the Court of the Iustices[61] at large: But if they be taken without any such point, yet the words, *Coram Iusticiariis ubicunq; fuerint*, doe set forth that other Court of the King, whereof I doe now entreat.

Lastly, I undertake to shew you, not by the *Title*, but by the *Text* of *Glanviles* owne Booke; that in his time the Kings Court was one, and the *Exchequer* was another: For throughout his whole Worke, hee [*30] calleth the Court of *Common Pleas, Curiam Domini Regis*, and the Stile of the *Writs* thereof is, *Quod sit coram me vel Iusticiariis meis;* but when he commeth to speake of the *Exchequer*, he talketh of Accompts to be made to the King there, and of none other matter; as namely, in the 7. Booke and 10. Chapter, where he hath this, *Si Dominus Rex aliquam Custodiam alicui commiserit, tunc distinguitur, utrum ei custodiam pleno jure commiserit: Ita*

---

[57] his] *F;* the *H BT.*

[58] de tempore] *F;* etc: Tempore *H BT.*

[59] spake] *F;* speaketh *H BT.*

[60] you] then you *F H BT.*

[61] Court . . . Iustices] *H;* Court of Iustice *F.*

[62] or] and *H.*

quod nullum inde reddere computum oportet[63] *ad Scaccarium aut aliter.*

The first beginning of[64] Iustices in Eyre.

But before that[65] I leave this King *Henry* the second, I must adde this also; That(†) he in the three and twentieth yeer of his Reign, did (by the advice of his Son and Bishops) [*31] cut the Realme into sixe parts, and to every of those parts appointed three *Iustices*, which by *Henry Bracton* are called *Itinerantes:* And in *Brittons* Booke *Iustices in Eyre, quasi errantes*, (As *Gervase* of *Tilbury* expoundeth it) in respect (as it seemeth) of those other which were first called *Residentes, Sedentes*,[66] and afterwards *de Banco*, for the reason of their certaine sitting[67] without remove.

The proper names of which *Iustices* are set downe by *Roger Hoveden*, who also describeth their circuits, not to differ much from the same that our *Iustices* of *Assize* doe now ride: and these *Iustices* held Plea as well of *criminall* as of *civill* Suits, and so continued till the beginning of the Reigne of King *Edward* the third, by which time their Authoritie was by little and little weakned, partly by a former advancing [*32] of certaine new *Iustices*, called of *Assize;* because their first Office was, to take *Assizes* of[68] *Mortdancester* and of *Novel Disseisin* (which in the customes of *Normandie*, from which it came, is called *La Novellette*)[68] in every Country: whereunto it was afterwards added, that they with others should take *Attaints*,

(†) *Math. Par. Ann.* 1176.

---

[63] computum oportet] compotum oportet *F;* compotum oporteat *H BT.*

[64] The first beginning of] *om. F;* The *H BT.*

[65] that] *BT; om. F H.*

[66] Sedentes,] or Sedentes, *H; om. F.*

[67] sitting] *F;* place of sitting *H.*

[68] of . . . Novellette] *H; om. F. BT omits this and more.*

Iuries, and *Certificats*, and deliver the Gaoles also; and partly by[69] erecting of *Wardens* of the *Peace* (afterwards called *Iustices* of the *Peace*) to whom likewise Iurisdiction of sundry sorts was given, and committed; so that about the beginning of the Reigne of King *Edward* the third, the Sessions in Eyr did altogether cease, and take leave.[70] And so I conclude, that not onely during all the time of the *Conqueror* himselfe, of *William* his Sonne, and of his other Sonne *Henry* (which was a peaceable Prince, and a maintainer [*33] of ancient *Lawes*, and learned in them; whereof he had the name *Beauclarke*) but also under the government of King *Stephen*, and of this *Henry* the second, there was one *High Court* following the King, which was the place of soveraigne *Iustice* both for matter of *Law* and *Conscience;* and one other standing *Court*, which was governesse onely of the *Land* and *Revenues* of the Crowne. The first of which, was then called *Curia Domini Regis*, and *Aula Regia;* for that the Prince himselfe did many times sit in person there, and had *Iustices a latere suo residentes*, (as *Bracton* saith) namely, his chiefe *Iustice*, *Chancellor*, *Constable*, *Marshall*, and others: for[71] which reason, it is called the *Bench* of the *King* even to this day.[71] The latter was then, as it is now, called *Scaccarium, eo quod lucibilis*[72] *Scaccarii formam haberet*, if you will give faith [*34] to *Gervase Tylburie;* or else it tooke the name of *Stattarium*, (as *Paulus Aemilius*, and after him *Polydor Virgil* doe write of it) or not unprobably[73] was called *Exchequer*, of *Escheats;* because it had the order of those things which the *Civilians* doe call *Caduca*, and we *Escheats*. And in this the Prince sate not personally at any time, but his chiefe *Iustice* as *President*, and then the *Chancelour* of the *Exchequer*, the *Treasurer*, and *Barons*.

---

[69] by] *H;* by the *F.*
[70] leave] *F;* their leave *H.*
[71] for . . . day] *H; om. F BT.*
[72] lucibilis] *F;* lusibilis *H BT.*
[73] not unprobably] *H; om. F.*

THE[74] COURT OF COMMON PLEAS.[74]

In[75] this plight that *High Court* of the King continued, untill that *Henry* the third, in the ninth yeare of his reigne, (which was about the time in which he aspired to the age of 21. yeares) finding by experience, that it was either chargeable or dilatorie, or both, for his subjects [*35] to have no other remedie for tryall of their *rights*, but either before himselfe, in that *Supreme Court*, (which removed with him wheresoever he went) or before those *Iustices* in *Eyre* (which came not yearely into the Countrie) granted unto his subjects that *great Charter* of the Liberties of *England;* in the 11. *Chapter* whereof, he ordained thus: *Communia Placita non sequantur Curiam nostram, sed teneantur in aliquo certo loco.* Whereupon followed two things: The first, that a new *Court* was erected for the determination of such *Pleas* as did not concerne the *Crowne* and *Dignitie* of the *Prince*, but were meerely *Civill*, and did belong to the subjects betweene themselves: The second, that this *Court* was established in a place certaine, and that was at *Westminster;* to the end, that the people might have a standing Seat of *Iustice*, [*36] whereunto they might resort, for the tryall of their owne *Causes*, and not be driven to follow the *King* and his *Court*, but onely where the matter respected him. And after this, all the Writs that are recited in *Henry Bractons* Booke, (which was written in the latter end of the reigne of this King *Henry* the third) have this *commandement* to the partie; *Quod sit coram Iusticiariis meis apud Westminster,*[76] and not *Coram me vel Iusticiariis meis*, as the former forme in *Glanvile* was. And thus began that *Court;* which, because it hath power over *Common Pleas*, wee now call the *Common Pleas.*[77]

---

[74] The . . . Pleas] *H; om. F;* The Commune Place *BT*.

[75] In] And in *F H BT*.

[76] Westminster] *F;* Westmonasterium *H BT*.

[77] Common Pleas] *F;* Common place *H BT*.

The division of the Courts by Britton.[78]

About this time also, (or not long after) some other *Courts* of *Iustice* were likewise opened, as [*37] it may partly appeare by *Henry Bracton*, but more plainely by *Iohn Britton*, who followed immediatly after him.

For in the Reign of King *Edward* the first, this *Iohn Britton*, then Bishop of *Hereford* (whose name Master *Bale* in his *Centuries*, or his *Printer* mistaketh, and calleth *Becton*) being singularly learned in the Lawes of the Realme, (did) at the commandement of that King, in[79] his name compile a Book, now imprinted, and named *Britton*, in the beginning whereof he parteth all Iurisdictions thus:

1 First, that the King himselfe hath soveraigne Iurisdiction above all others in his Realme, to judge of all causes whatsoever.

2 Secondly, that the (†)*Marshall* of the Kings House have the place of the King, to heare and determine *Pleas*[80] of the Crowne within the [*38] *Verge*, and that the *Iustices in Eyre* have like Authoritie in every countrie once in seven yeeres.

3 Thirdly, that the Iustices shall[81] follow the King, wheresoever he goeth, and sit in his place, have Connuzance of *erroneous Iudgements*, *Appeales*, and other matters concerning the Crowne.

4 Fourthly, that the *Coroner* of the Household have his proper power within his[82] *Verge*, and that he and others have the order of *Weight* and *Measure* throughout the Realme.

5 Then that *Sheriffes*, *Coroners*, *Hundreders*, *Burgesses*,

(†) *Marshal* of *Mars*, *Marshal* of *Mare* a Horse, and *Shalke* a Governour, that is, Master of the Horse.

---

[78] by Britton] *H;* of Britaine *F. BT has as heading* The Booke called Britton.

[79] in] *F;* and in *H BT.*

[80] Pleas] *F;* the pleas *H BT.*

[81] shall] *F;* which *H BT.*

[82] his] *F;* the *H BT.*

Serjeants, and *Beadles*, have their Courts within every their particular limits.

6 Sixthly, that *Iustices* (being continually at *Westminster*) have[83] Authoritie concerning the Kings *Debts*, and *Fees*, and all things incident thereunto.

[*39] And lastly, that other *Iustices* have the charge of *Assizes*, and of the deliverie of Goales in every *Countie*.

And forasmuch as after this distribution of power thus made to hold Plea, some of these Courts would not containe themselves within their appointed limits, but sought to enlarge their Authoritie by usurping Iurisdiction that was appropriate to others, the same King did by Parliament (holden the 28. yeere of his Reigne) confirme the great Charter for ever, and in certaine Articles(†) (as he called them) set forth upon the Charter, did then by like Authoritie of Parliament, enact, that they of the *Exchequer* should not take knowledge of any *common Plea*; that the (‡)*Seneschall*, or *Steward*, and the *Marshall* of the Kings Houshold should not hold Plea of Frank tenement, [*40] but content themselves with the hearing of *Trespasses*, *Contracts*, and *Covenants*, made within the *Verge*, and that the *Chancellor* and the *Iustices* of the *Kings Bench* should follow him wheresoever he went, to the end he might alwayes have men about him, that were able to deliver *Law* to such as should require it.

Hitherto as you see, there is no expresse mention in *Britton*, either of the Court of the *Admiraltie*, the *Constables* Court, or of the *Chancerie*. Therefore it remaineth yet, that wee labour to find out from whence they also fetched their beginning.

(†) *Cap.* 3. 4. *&* 5.

(‡) *Seneschall*, of *Sein*, a house, and *Schale*, a Governor: So *Steward* of *Stow*, a house, *Ward* a Keeper.

---

[83] at Westminster) have] *F H;* at Westminster have power over commune pleas. Seventhly, that the Escheaquer at Westminster have *BT*.

And that shall we the more easily doe, if we give heed to this that *Britton* hath already opened; for he leaveth the *soveraigne Iurisdiction* of all Causes in the King: So that whatsoever the King hath not particularly [*41] delivered out to others, his Iustices *Commissioners* and *Delegats* that still remained in himselfe, and was exercised either by himselfe in person, or by his *Chancellor, Counsellors* of Estate, and *Iustices* of Law that continually attended upon himselfe for that service.

THE ADMIRALTIE, AND ITS NAME.[84]

And therefore, first concerning the *Admiraltie*, I thinke that the decision of *marine* Causes was not put out of the Kings House, and committed over to the charge of the *Admirall*, untill the time of King *Edward* the third, whereunto I am led partly by the consideration of the time of his Reign, which was much occupied with affaires beyond the Sea, both by reason of the[85] warres in *France*, and of the Entercourse [*42] and Trade of Merchandize which then flourished, and partly for that I finde no mention of the *Admiralty* before the second yeere of the Reigne of King *Richard* the second, who going about (by a *Statute* made in the 13. yeere after his comming to the Crowne) to restraine the authoritie of that Court (which had exceeded her knowne limits, doth take order that shee doth[86] meddle no further than she wonted to doe in the time of his grandfather King *Edward* the third, thereby reducing her *authoritie* (as I thinke) to the first originall.

Admirall. 'Αλμυρίς.[87]

This *Admirall* hath the name of the *Greeke* word 'Αλμυραρχη; which being declined, and fallen from *Almurar* to *Almurall*, as Doctor *Caius* (our Country-man, following

[84] Admiraltie, and its name] Admirals Court *F H;* Admiraltie *BT.*
[85] the] *F;* his *H BT.*
[86] doth] *F;* should *H BT.*
[87] Admirall. 'Αλμυρίς.] *om. F;* The word Admyrall *H.*

Paulus Aemilius, writeth) doth signifie the *Governour*, or *Captaine* of the Navie.

[*43] The Constables Court, and whence the Name.[88]

The Court of the *Constable*, or[89] *Marshall* of *England*, determineth Contracts touching deeds of *Armes* out of the Realme, and handleth things concerning *Warre* within the Realme, as *Combats*, *Blazon*, *Armorie*, &c. but it may not deale with *Battaile* in *Appeales*, nor generally with any other thing that may be tryed by the Lawes of the Land.

And albeit that *Britton* (whose purpose was only to set forth the Courts whereof there was common use) hath not numbred it among the Courts of that time, yet I doe verily beleeve, that it came hither with the *Conqueror* out of *Normandie:* for amongst other *Lawes* of his, this is one.

[*44] That if a *French man* doe appeale an *English man* of perjurie or murder, the *French man* may defend himselfe by *Battaile*, which was then termed in *English*, *Ernest;*[90] a word that we keep yet, saying, when wee see a man fight, hee is an *Ernest:*[91] And forasmuch as the thing it selfe was then (and never before) permitted by *Law*, it is to be granted, that there was even then also some *Officer* who had the charge to see it performed according to *Law*, who no doubt was the *Constable*, as it may well appeare, not onely by some *Records* of *Historie*, but also by a speciall *President* that I have seene concerning the whole order of proceeding in that behalfe before him: this man also had the name of *Connestable*, as *Iohannes Tullius* thinketh, of the *Latin* word *Comestabilis*, *quasi comes stabuli*, that is, *Archippocomes*, or the Master of the *Horse*, as

---

[88] and whence the Name] *om. F BT. H omits the entire heading, but near the end of this section has* The word Connestable.

[89] , or] *F;* & *H BT.*

[90] Ernest] *F;* Eornest *H BT.*

[91] an Ernest] *F;* in earnest *H BT.*

wee [*45] speake: but as *Iohannes Goropius* affirmeth, the word *Constable* (or rather *Conning stable*) is derived of *Conning*, that is to say, a *King*, and of *Stable*,[92] which signifieth a *Proppe*, or *Stay;* because the *Constable* (being a principall Personage neere unto the *King*) is a great stay and aid unto him.

The Chancellor and Chancerie Court.

But now as touching the *Chancellor*, (because I purpose to speake of him and his *Court* somewhat more largely) it shall not be amisse, first to derive his Name, then to divide his Authoritie and Office; and after that, to search for the beginning of him, and his *Court:* and lastly, to speake a word or twaine of the *Equitie* by which he is said to rule his *Sentence.*

[*46] Our(†) *French* word *Chancellier*, is fetched from the *Latine*, *Cancellarius;* and that, from *cancello;* and they all three framed out of the *Greeke* Καγκαλῶ; which signifieth properly, to make *Lattises*, *Grates*, or *Crosse-barres*, to enclose any thing withall; and *metaphorically*, to bound and containe any thing within certaine *barres* and *limits.*

And out of these two significations, two principall parts of his *Office* doe issue: For after the similitude to[93] those *crossed Barres* or *Lattises*, he is said to *cancell*, *deface*, or *make void* a *Record*, because the *vacat* thereof is done, by drawing certaine crosse lines Lattise-wise with his Pen over it; whereby it is so inclosed and shut up, that from thenceforth no exemplifications thereof may be given abroad.

And likewise in his *Court* of *Equitie*, he doth (when the Case requireth) [*47] so *cancell* and *shut up* the *rigour* of the

(†) The name of *Chancellor*, *Carol. Steph. in Dictionar. Latinograec. ex Budaei vigiliis.*

---

[92] Stable] *F;* Staple *H BT.*

[93] to] of *F H BT.*

generall *Law*, that it shall not breake forth to the hurt of some one singular Case and person.

The great[94] Seale, and the Office of him that beareth it.[94]

The *Office* and *Iurisdiction* of this man, is manifold: For usually he is a great *Personage*, a *Counsellor* of the *Estate*, and *Prolocutor* or *Mouth* of the higher House of *Parliament:* He is also *Keeper* of the *Great Seale* of the King, and was wont to be elected hereunto by authoritie of *Parliament*.

For I have read,(†) that *Ralph Nevil*, the Bishop of *Chichester*, being *Chancellor* to King *Henry* the third, refused to yeeld up his[95] *Seale* unto him, when he required it; affirming, that as hee had received it by the *Common Councell* of the *Realme*, so hee [*48] would not, without like *Warrant*, resigne it againe; And in the dayes of the same King, it was told him by all his Lords *spirituall* and *temporall*, That of ancient time the *Creation* and *Deposition* of the *chiefe Iustice*, the *Chancellor*, and the *Treasurer*, belonged to the *Parliament*.(‡)

And besides this *Seale* of speciall Grace, the *Chancellor* hath also the *Seale* of simple *Iustice*, and keepeth (as it were) the *Forge* and *Shop* of all *Originals*.(††)

He hath moreover double *Iurisdiction;* the one, of *Common Law;* the other, of *Equitie;* that first being limitted in power, and his[96] latter being meere absolute, and infinite.

According to the Rule of *Law*, he holdeth *Plea* (by Bill in *Latine*) for[97] *priviledge* of the *ministers* of his *Court*, and their *attendants*. So also upon *Recognizances, Statutes, Audita* [*49]

(†) *Math. Par.*
(‡) 7. *H.* 7. 15. *Comment.* 76.
(††) *Stanf. Prerog.* 65.*a.*

---

[94] The great . . . it] *om. F;* The great Seale *H BT.*
[95] his] *F;* the *H BT.*
[96] his] *F;* this *H BT.*
[97] for] *F;* for the *H BT.*

querela, Petitions, Monstrans de Droit: and so of *Wards, Liveries,* and *Ouster le main,* before a speciall Court was erected therefore. And of these he may hold *Plea* at all times, as well within the *Terme,* as after.(†) According to his *Conscience* (guided by *Equitie*) hee relieveth those that complaine (by *English Bill*) either for that the *Common Law* oppresseth[98] them with rigour, or else for that it hath not fit medicine for their diseases and griefe. Hitherto of the Name of[99] *Office* of the *Chancellor.*

Now for the better understanding of the beginning of them both, wee will examine the matter by parts: And first, for his originall dutie, I will use one or two testimonies of Antiquitie.

King *Edward* the *Confessor* immediately before his *death,* granted by his *Charter* many Possessions and Priviledges to the *Abbey* that was [*50] called Saint *Peters,* in *Westminster;* in the conclusion of which *Charter,* he saith thus: *Ad ultimum Chartam istam sigillari jussi, & ipse manu mea propria Signum X Crucis impressi, & idoneos testes annotari praecepi.* And then, after the Subscription of *Him* and the *Queene,* and after the *Archbishops, Bishops,* and *Abbots,* one *Reinbaldus* is named *Cancellarius.* And in the end of all, after the Date of the *Charter,* it is written thus: *Siwardus Notarius ad vicem Reinbaldi Regiae dignitatis Cancellarii hanc Chartam scripsi, & subscripsi.*

After this, King *William* the *Conquerour* gave, by another *Charter,* to the same *Abbey* sundry Lands in exchange for *Windsor,* which King *Edward* had bestowed upon them: And in the end of this *Grant* hee likewise saith; *Ego Willielmus Dei gratia Rex, & Dux Normaniorum,*[1] *atque Princeps Caenomanorum hoc scribi* [*51] *praecepi, & scriptum hoc signo Domi-*

(†) *Fitz. Nat. Bre.* 261.

---

[98] oppresseth] *F;* presseth *H BT.*
[99] of] *F;* and *H BT.*
[1] Normaniorum] *F;* Normanorum *H BT.*

nicae Crucis X confirmando stabilivi, nostraeque imaginis sigillo insuper assignari curavi: And then (in order as before) it followeth; *Ego Mauricius Regis Cancellarius favendo relegi & sigillavi.* Hereby it appeareth, that the *Office* of the *Chancellor* then was, at the first, to *make* and *seale* the *Instruments* that passed from the *Prince.*

And this I call his *Originall Dutie*, because it cannot be credibly shewed out of any *Historie* (as I thinke) that ever there was in *England* any sealing of *Writings*, or mention of the Name of *Chancellor*, before the dayes of this *Edward;* who having spent a great part of his age in *Normandie*, first brought the use of the *Seale* from thence into this *Realme;* and with it (as I suppose) the Name of *Chancellor* also. In (†) whose time also, *Leofricus* the *Brittaine* is the first that I find named *Chancellor.* [*52] For, that we learned of the *Normans* our manner of sealing, *Ingulphus* the *Abbot* of *Croyland*, (which came out of *Normandie* hither, in the traine of the *Norman Conquerour*) assureth us in writing thus: *Normani Chiragraphorum confectionem cum crucibus aureis, & aliis signaculis sacris in Anglia firmari solitam in caerae impressionem mutabit,*[2] *&c.* And that the Name of him that kept this *Seale*, came out of *France* also, it may be probably conjectured, both by the words[3] which wee found neerer to the pronuntiation of the *French*, than of the *Latine;* and also by the *Office* it selfe, which hath beene exercised in *France* (under the very same name and nature that wee use it) ever since the time of *Charlemaine* at the least. (‡)

And so it is manifest, that the *Chancellor* did beare this Name, and had this charge of the Kings *Seale*, [*53] and *Writings*, both before and in the time of the *Conquerour:* The

(†) *Florent. Wigor.*
(‡) *Vincent. sup.* [*Lup.*] *l.* 2. *de Gall. Magist.*

---

[2] mutabit] *F;* mutant *H BT.* [3] words] *F;* word *H BT.*

which also, without all doubt, he hath ever since continued.

Howbeit, when I say *Writings*, I doe not meane that he had the authoritie of making originall *Writs* here, before the time of the *Conquest:* For those came out of *Normandie* also, as the very formes of the most of them (being expressed in the Booke of the *Norman* Customes) may lead a man to thinke. And that the rather, because the *Saxons* (our Ancestors) whose proceeding in Iudgement was *de plano*, and without *solemnitie*, did not use (so farre as I have hitherto observed) to call the parties by any *Writ*, or *Writing*, but to send for them by certaine *Messengers*, which they tearmed (†)*Theignes;* that is to say, *Ministers*, or *Servants:* even as in the *Norman* Customes, it seemeth that they [*54] sent *Sergeants*, without originall *Writs*, or *Mandate* in *writing*. Yea, and when that manner of summoning by *Writ* was brought into use[4] here, yet was not the sealing of the *Writs* forthwith committed to the *Chancellor:* For you may see in *Glanviles* Booke, that the originall *Writs* of this time had this forme; *Teste Ranulpho de Glanvillo, &c.* which was the name of the *Chiefe Iustice* of the Kings Courts then, under whose sealings they passed abroad.

Neverthelesse, for as much as it is to be read in *Bracton, Quod omnia brevia de pace* (which are *Prohibitions* indeed) *irrotulari debent in Rotulo de Cancellaria;* and for that, not onely the Statute of *Westminster* the second, which was made in the thirteenth yeere of King *Edward* the first, saith in plaine words, that the *Formedone in Reverter satis est in* [*55] *usu in Cancellaria*, and hath often mention of the *Clerks* there; but also that other Statute of *Articuli super Chartas*, hath the ex-

(†) Which signifies, *famulus & minister: Ic Thein*, by the corrupting of one *Saxon* Letter, is that which is the *Motto* at this day of the Princes Plume.

---

4 use] *H BT;* use and custome *F.*

presse names both of the *Chancellor*, and *Chancerie:* It must be confessed, that the *Chancellor* had the keeping of the *Rolls* of *Record*, and the making out of *Writs* originall, either at the same time that the *Common Place* was erected, or not long after it; that is to say, either under the Reigne of King *Henry* the third, or else in the beginning of *Edward* the first: Which later King (as Iudge *Prisot* reporteth of him) laboured carefully to reduce our *Law* into order, and writing; and in my opinion, may therefore not unworthily bee accounted our *English Iustinian*.

And (†) albeit the House of the *Rolls* (which hath beene of long time, as it were, the *Colledge* of the *Chancerie-men*) [*56] was builded at the first by the same King *Henry* the third for another purpose; namely, for the sustentation of such *Iewes* as would give their names to *Christ*, and was therefore called *Domus Iudaeorum conversorum:* yet that hindereth not, but that the same House might shortly after be converted to another use; upon experience, as it is likely, that few *Converts* were found amongst the *Iewes*, for to inhabite it.

And then, thus have you the *Chancellor* furnished with the *Seale* of *Grace*, and *Seale* of *Common Iustice;* and with him the *Chancerie*, for the keeping of *Records;* and the *Clerkes* thereof, for the framing of *Writs*.

And as touching the Authoritie in *Iudgement*, I see not what *Iurisdiction* hee hath, (his Court of *Equitie*, and some powers given by [*57] late Statutes only excepted) which is not incident to the making or keeping of the *Records:* For hee cannot reforme[5] the error of another Court; yea, error committed in his owne Court, shall be reversed in the *Parliament:* (‡) Neyther can hee trie any *Issue*, taken before him; for that

(†) *Math. Par.*
(‡) 37. *H.* 6. 14. *&* 15.

---

[5] reforme] *H BT;* forgive *F.*

also must be done in the *Kings Bench*, as a thing without his *Iurisdiction.*(†) And that moved *Scroope, Chiefe Iustice* of the *Kings Bench*, (as I have seene) *Mi.* 1. *Edward* 3. in a written *Report* to say, That the *Chancerie* and the *Kings Bench* were but one place, *viz.* the *Bench* of the King; and that the *Chancellor* may (by his *Hand*, without *Writ*) deliver any thing to be tryed in the *Bench* of the King.

[*58] THE[6] COURT OF EQUITIE, OR CHANCERIE.[6]

It remaineth then, that I speake of his Court of *Equitie;* which, in my fantasie, is not altogether so ancient as the other: For, as you have heard before, King *Edward* the first, and the *Parliament*, then tooke order, That the *Chancellor* should follow the King, even as the *Iudges*[7] of the *Bench* did; to the end, that he might have alwayes at hand able men for his direction in *Suits* that came before him.

The meaning whereof (as I think) was, That the *Iustices* should informe him of the *Law*, and the *Chancellor* of *Equitie:* For otherwise, I see not what use he could have of the *Chancellor* in this behalfe; but onely, for that hee (being commonly a *Bishop*, or other Spirituall person) [*59] was the more meet (after the opinion of men in those dayes) to give advice according to *Equitie*, and a good[8] *Conscience;* in which respect also hee was *Visitor* for the King, and bestowed his *Benefices:* So that, such as then sought reliefe by *Equitie*, were suitors to the King himselfe, who being assisted with his *Chancellor* and Councell,[9] did mitigate the severitie of the[10] *Law* in his owne person, when it pleased him to be present; and did (in

(†) *Scire facias, Fitzh.* 129.

---

[6] The . . . Chancerie] *om. F;* The Chancery Court for Equity *H;* The Channcerie Courte *BT.*
[7] Iudges] *F;* Iustices *H BT.*
[8] a good] *F;* good *H; om. BT.*
[9] his Chancellor and Councell] *H BT;* the Chancellor, himselfe *F.*
[10] the] *F; om. H BT.*

absence) either referre the same[11] to the *Chancellor* alone, or to him and some other of the Councell: So,[12] as the *Chancellor* had not then any Court proper to himself, but rather assisted the King (as then did the *Chiefe Iustice*, and the rest of the Kings Councell also) or otherwise supplyed the Kings absence, by special *commandement*, for deciding of *Causes* that had been presented to his royall person.

[*60] For when as King *Edward* the first, in his Booke commonly called *Britton*, (which he caused to be penned about the first part of his reign, by the labour of learned *Iudges*, in the vulgar *French*, for the better publication of the *Lawes*, which then stood written in *Latine* by *Glanvile* and *Bracton*) had set downe all the sorts of Lay *Iurisdiction;* beginning his distribution at the highest (even his owne Princely *Tribunall*) and ending with the lowest *Leet*, and common *Court Baron:* Wherein also he laboureth (as it seemeth) to peruse all, and pretermit none: Yet speaketh he never a word touching any *Iurisdiction* of a *Chancerie* Court; albeit the *Chancellor* were then one of the neerest of his Councell, and did not onely attend him with advice, but did also keepe his sacred Seale, and exercised therewith the awarding of all the Kings originall [*61] *Writs*, whereupon the rest of his Courts of *Iustice* did worke, and proceed. Yea, it is probable also, that either then, or soone after, it rested in the *Chancellors* power to devise any *Writ* for the direction of *Suits* at the *Common Law*, for remedie in *Cases*, where no proper helpe was formerly knowne. The doing whereof (conformed to the Authoritie of the *Roman Praetors*) was extraordinarie, and speciall; and was therefore then, and yet is called the *Action* or *Writ* upon the *Case;* as by the benefit whereof, the *Suitor* in *Law* might have readie reliefe, according to the

---

11 the same] *H;* it *F BT.*

12 *F and BT both omit what follows (this sentence and the next six paragraphs) as far as p. *65.*

exigencie of his businesse, and fitting to the *Specialtie*, *Reason*, and *Equitie* of his very *Case*.

And here[13] it is, that our *Register* affordeth so plentifull varietie of *Writs* upon the *Case*, warranted by the Statute of *Westminster* the second, [*62] saying in the first and 25. Chapter, *In novo casu, novum remedium est apponendum; ne*[14] *Curia Domini Regis deficiat, conquaerentibus in justitia perquirenda.*

And[15] thus I take the matter to have stood, during such time as the Kings high[16] Court of *Iustice* accompanied his Royall presence.

But when as afterwards the Court of the *Kings Bench* was left to it selfe (the King no longer frequenting the same in person) and therewithall, the Authoritie of the *Chiefe Iustice* of *England* (who formerly had, as a Vice-roy, the absolute Royall power, as well of matters[17] of *Estate*, as for *Warre* and civill *Iustice*) did cease, and decline from that originall greatnesse, and was restrained by a new forme of *Patent* (as now it stands) *ad placita coram nobis tenenda*, which is an ordinarie and limitted *Iurisdiction:* Then, I say, the King [*63] did commit to his *Chancellor* (together with the charge of the great *Seale*) his owne Regall, absolute, and extraordinarie preheminence of *Iurisdiction* in *Civill* Causes, as well for amendment as for supply of the *Common Law*. And therefore this great *Officer* doth beare sundry apparant markes, by the which hee is plainely knowne and distinguished from whatsoever *Iudges:*[18] For hee is the Mouth, as it were, of the Prince, as appeares by his imployment in the[19] Session of *Parliament:* he commandeth the whole great *Seale*, whereas other Courts

---

[13] here] hence *H.*

[14] ne] Et concordent clerici de cancellaria in Brevi faciundo ne *H.*

[15] *Here H has as section heading:* The absolute Authoritie of the Chancellor.

[16] high] *om. H.*

[17] of matters] for matter *H.*

[18] Iudges] other Iudges *H.*

[19] the] each *H.*

doe use onely a part thereof; acknowledging thereby, their derived Authoritie underneath him.

This *Seale* he holdeth (without any *Patent*) by the onely deliverie thereof into his hands: He writeth, *Teste me ipsa*, in the name and person of the Queene her selfe; when the [*64] other *Iudges* say, *Teste Iohanne Popham, Edmundo Anderson*, or *Willielmo Periam:* His Court is said to be alwayes open, and (touching *Equitie*) to have no *Record;* as well because extraordinarie *Cases* may not be limitted to any times certaine, as for that his *Iudgements* be in his owne brest, not tyed to any preceding *Records:* Neither doth he trie any *Issue*, because he may examine both *parties* and *witnesses* upon *Oath*, and may (without judiciall Ceremonie) judge *summarie & de plano;* therefore also his Sentence bindeth not the thing judged. His *Supersedeas* may not stay a Court of *Common Iustice* from proceeding; neyther doth a *Scire facias* lye, for the summe contained in the *Subpoena*, when it is not obeyed; because his power is singular, and of it selfe, which may rule the person which is commandable by the absolute and [*65] Regall *Iustice* of the Prince, where no ordinarie *Law* is yet provided.

And even as the necessitie of an *Officer* of this sort is inevitable in every well-polliced[20] *Kingdome*, where the Prince is by *Office* bounden and by *Oath* sworne to deliver *Iustice* to his subjects, howsoever the *Positive Law* of his Countrie doth not afford it; so hath this manner of *Iurisdiction* here beene both approved and enlarged by sundry *Lawes* of *Parliament.*

For, when as King *Edward* the third prepared for his Warres in France, it was enacted in the twentieth yeere of his Reigne,[21] That the *Chancellor* and *Treasurer* should heare

[20] well-polliced] well policyed *H.*

[21] *F (like BT and unlike H) omits more than six paragraphs up to this point, opening this paragraph with:* And this continued (if I be not deceived) untill the twentieth yeare of the Reigne of King Edward 3, in which yeare when he made preparation for his Warre upon France, it was enacted by Parliament.

and[22] determine upon *Extortions*, *Embraceries*, *Maintenances*, and other[23] like offences that[24] should be committed in this Kings absence. In which,[24] albeit (as[25] you see) the *Power* given was absolute,[25] yet was not[26] the [*66] *Chancellor* made the onely *Iudge*:[26] But afterwards[27] (in the 36. yeere of the same King)[28] it was enacted,[29] That if any man were grieved against[30] the Articles of that Statute,[31] or others, he[32] should have remedie in the *Chancerie*, without further or[33] other suit: And[34] hereby hee was not onely to judge alone, but also at the libertie of his owne discretion.[34]

Sundry[35] other accessions of honour were after that also given by sundry Statutes:[35] As by one, to award *Damages* upon an untrue suggestion made before him: By another, to send *Proclamation* of *Rebellion* against such as by *contumacie*[36] would not appeare, when[37] *Processe* had been awarded against them:[37] And by other *Lawes*,[38] to grant *Commissions* of sun-

---

22 heare and] *H; om. F BT.*

23 upon Extortions, Embraceries, Maintenances, and other] *H;* all Complaints against extortion of Officers, mainetenance, imbracery, and such *F BT.*

24 that . . . which] *H;* And *F BT.*

25 (as . . . absolute] *H;* that indeed this Authority bee neither granted to himselfe alone, nor doth plainely erect any Court of Equity *F BT.*

26 was not . . . Iudge] *H;* for asmuch as it is the first severall power of this sort, that I finde committed unto him from the King, in which also it is to be thought, that the proceeding was extraordinary, and absolute even as the Kings owne before was: I suppose it to be the laying of the first stone of the Chancery Court *F BT* (*BT reads* stone of the foundation of the Channcelours Courte).

27 afterwards] *H;* after this *F BT.*

28 King] *H;* Kings Reigne *F BT.*

29 enacted] provided *H;* provided by Parliament *F BT.*

30 against] *H;* contrary to *F BT.*

31 Statute] *H;* Parliament *F BT.*

32 he] *H;* then hee *F;* that he *BT.*

33 further or] *H; om. F BT.*

34 And . . . discretion] *H;* By which Law the Chancellor was not only made sole Judge in this newly erected Court, but was enabled also to proceed in iudgement there after his own discretion: for otherwise the words without other suite were not beneficiall *F BT* (*F actually reads* in iudgement thereafter by his owne).

35 Sundry . . . Statutes] *H;* After this also his Authority was from time to time enlarged by sundry Parliaments *F BT.*

36 by contumacie] *H; om. F BT.*

37 when . . . them] *H; om. F BT.*

38 other Lawes,] *H;* others, both *F BT.*

dry[39] kinds, and to doe and dispatch many Businesses;[40] whereof it is neither needfull nor profitable[41] to make enumeration[42] or report in this [*67] place;[42] where[43] I doe rather seeke[44] to finde the *Originall*, than follow the *Off-spring;* to taste of the *Well-head*, rather than pursue the *Channell.*

That I may therefore change this path, and make choice of another; even[43] as these be the first, the[45] beginnings, (that hitherto[46] I can finde amongst our *Statute-Lawes*)[47] concerning this preheminent[48] *Authoritie* of the *Chancerie* Court; so also I doe not remember, that in our *Reports* of *Common Law* there is any frequent[49] mention of *Causes* usually drawne[50] before the *Chancellor*, for helpe in *Equitie*, but onely from the time of King *Henry* the fourth; in whose dayes (by reason of those intestine troubles) *Feoffements* to *Use*[51] did either first begin (as some hath thought) or else did first grow common and familiar, as all men must agree.

For remedie in which Cases of *Uses*, chiefely the *Chancerie* Court [*68] was then fled unto, as the only *Altar* of helpe and refuge: But whensoever this Court of *Equitie* tooke beginning to be a distinct Court, I have made proofe (as I thinke) that the power thereof was alwayes in exercise.

And[52] considering that the *Prince* of this *Realme* is the immediate *minister* of *Iustice* under *God*, and is sworne at his *Coronation*, to deliver to his subjects *aequam & rectam Iustitiam;* I cannot see how it may otherwise be, but that besides

---

39 sundry] *H;* divers *F BT.*

40 and dispatch many Businesses] *H;* many other things *F BT.*

41 neither needfull nor profitable] *H;* not needful *F BT.*

42 enumeration . . . place] *H;* rehearsal here *F BT.*

43 where . . . even] *H;* And truly, *F BT.*

44 seeke] labour *H.*

45 first, the] first *F H BT.*

46 hitherto] *H; om. F BT.*

47 amongst our Statute-Lawes] *H;* in Statute-law *F BT.*

48 preheminent] *H; om. F BT.*

49 any frequent] much *H;* any *F BT.*

50 usually drawne] *H; om. F;* drawen *BT.*

51 Use] *F;* uses *H BT.*

52 *H here has as section heading:* Necessity of a Court of Equitie.

his Court of meere *Law*, he must either reserve to himselfe, or referre to others a certaine soveraigne and preheminent *Power*, by which he may both supply the want, and correct the rigour of that *Positive* or *written Law*, which of it selfe neither is nor can be made such a perfect *Rule*, as that a *Man* may thereby truly square out *Iustice* in all *Cases* that may happen.

[*69] For *written Lawes* must needs bee made in a generalitie, and be grounded upon that which happeneth for the most part,(†) because no wisdome of man can fore-see every thing in particularitie, which Experience and Time doth beget.

And therfore, although the *written Law* be generally good, and just; yet in some speciall case, it may have need of Correction,(‡) by reason of some considerable Circumstance falling out afterwards, which at the time of the Law-making was not fore-seene: Whereas otherwise, to apply one generall Law to all particular cases, were to make all *Shooes* by one *Last*, or to cut one *Glove* for all *Hands*, which how unfit it would prove, every man may readily perceive. And hereof this *Equitie* hath the name in *Greek* 'επιειϰια, of 'επι *secundum*, and 'ειϰος *conveniens, vel rationi consentaneum;* because it [*70] doth not onely weigh what is generally meet for the most part, but doth also consider, the person, time, place, and other circumstances in every singular case that commeth in question, and doth thereof frame such judgement as is convenient and agreeable to the same: So that in sum the *written Law* is like to a stiffe rule of *Steel*, or *Iron*, which will not be applied to the fashion of the *Stone* or *Timber* whereunto it is laid: And *Equitie* (as *Aristotle* saith well) is like to the leaden rule of the *Lesbian Artificers*, which they might at pleasure bend, and bow to every stone of whatsoever fashion. And[53] hereby it may also

(†) *Leges habent se ut universalia ad singularia.* Aristot. Ethic. 5.
(‡) *Ipsae etiam Leges cupiunt ut iure regantur.* Cato.

[53] *H here has as section heading:* Use of a Courte of Equitye.

appeare, what use there ought to be aswell of the *Positive* or *Written Law*, as also of *Equitie* it selfe: For seeing that the *Positive* and *Common Law* is made meet for the most part, and that *Equitie* is added for helpe in [*71] some few or singular cases, it followeth by reason, that commonly and regularly the *positive Law* should bee put in ure, and that *Equitie* should not[54] bee appealed unto but only in rare and extraordinary matters, lest on the one side, if the *Iudge* in *Equitie* should take *Iurisdiction* over all, it should come to passe (as *Aristotle* saith) that a *Beast* should beare the rule: For so hee calleth man, whose *Iudgement*, if it bee not restrained by the Chaine of *Law*, is commonly carried away, with unruly affections. And on the other side, if onely streight Law should bee administred, the helpe of *GOD* which speaketh in that *Oracle* of *Equitie*, should be denyed unto men that neede it. And therefore even as two *Herbes* being in extremitie of heat, or cold, bee by themselves so many [*72] poysons, and[55] if they bee skilfully contempered, will make a wholesome *Medicine:* So also would it come to passe, if either this *Arithmeticall Governement*, (as they call it) by rigour of *Law* onely, or this *Geometricall Iudgement* at the pleasure of the *Chancellour* or *Praetor* onely should bee admitted; and yet if they bee well compounded together, a most sweete and harmonicall *Iustice* will follow of them. A[56] good *Chancellor* will not then[57] make this Proclamation, *Nullus recedat a Cancellaria sine remedio*, and thereby[58] not onely abuse the Text of the Statute, which meant onely the making of *Writs* (that there might bee *in consimile casu remedium consimile*) but also arrogate authoritie in[58] every complaint that shall bee brought[59] [*73]

---

[54] not] *om. F H BT.*

[55] and] and yet *F H BT.*

[56] *H here has as section heading:* Abuse of the Court of Equitie.

[57] will not then] *F;* then will not now *H BT.*

[58] thereby . . . authoritie in] *H;* so receive knowledge of *F BT* (*F actually reads* received).

[59] brought] *H;* made *F BT.*

before him, upon whatsoever suggestion, and[60] thereby both overthrow the authoritie[60] of the Courts of *Common Law:* Then to bring[61] upon men such a[62] confusion and uncertainetie, as hardly any man should[63] know how, or how long to[64] hold his owne assured to him.[65] Nay rather a good *Chancellour* will permit[66] the *Common Law* to hold[67] her just honour, and not make such violent irruption[68] upon her borders, but will so moderate his power, and[68] provide, that the Gate of *Mercie* may bee opened in all Calamitie of Suit: to the end,[69] (where need shall bee) the Rigour of *Law* may bee amended, and[70] the short measure thereof extended by the true consideration of *Iustice* and[70] *Equitie.* In which behalfe this our Age hath greatly to thanke *God*, for that by the ministerie [*74] of our gracious *Queene Elizabeth*, hee doth not onely leave unto us the right use of those *Courts* of meere *Law*, furnished[71] with men of greater learning and integritie,[71] but hath also by her own selection[72] placed in that *Praetoriall Seat* of[73] *Chancerie*,

---

[60] and . . . authoritie] *F BT;* tendinge no lesse to the overthrow *H.*

[61] Then to bring] *H;* and also bring in *F BT.*

[62] men such a] *F BT;* all men such *H.*

[63] should] *H;* shall *F BT.*

[64] how long to] *H;* when he may *F BT.*

[65] to him] unto him *H; om. F BT. H alone hereupon inserts the following:* For as it is Common to all Courts to amplifie their owne Iurisdictions, Soe if this great Iudge should not refuse manie things offered by Complaint of Suitors, who durst refuse, and take excepcion to his growinge greatnes? yea it would come soe to passe, in the preiudice of the ordinary Lawe, and vexacion of the Subiect, That it might seeme a good question and worthie Discourse, whether it be more sufferable and Convenient to have noe Courte of Equitie att all, or to have it of soe exorbitant and overflowinge Authoritie.

[66] Nay rather a good Chancellour will permit] *H;* but he will rather suffer *F BT.*

[67] hold] *H;* have *F BT.*

[68] make such violent irruption . . . power, and] make anie such vyolent interrupcion . . . power and *H;* to be interrupted in her right course; and will yet withall *F BT.*

[69] end] *F;* end that *H BT.*

[70] and . . . Iustice and] *H;* by the Iudgement of *F BT.*

[71] furnished . . . integritie] *H; om. F BT.*

[72] by her own selection] *H;* hitherto *F BT.*

[73] Seat of] *H;* Roome, or *F BT.*

a man[74] no lesse learned in[75] the *Common Lawes* of this Realme,[76] than accomplished[77] with the skill of this *Moderation* for *Equitie.*[78]

I[79] see that occasion is here offered me, to enter into the handling of sundry Questions concerning the Order of the *Chancerie*, and chiefly of this one thing: whether it be meet, that the *Chancellor* shold appoint unto himselfe, and publish to others any certaine *Rules* & *Limits* of *Equity*, or no; about the which men both godly and learned doe varie in opinion: For on the one part it is thought as hard a thing to prescribe to *Equitie* any [*75] certaine bounds, as it is to make any one generall Law to be a meet measure of *Iustice* in all particular cases. And on the other side it is said, that if it be not knowne before-hand in what cases the *Chancellour* will reach forth his helpe, and where not, then neither shall the Subject bee assured how, or when he may possesse his owne in peace, nor the Practizer in *Law* be able to informe his Client what may become of his Action: But because this and the like matters be of more difficultie then that I may with modestie take upon me to determine them, and for that also it is not my present purpose to dispute what is convenient to bee done in any Court, but rather to discourse the beginning, and acknowledge the benefit of them all, I will onely wish these two things. First, some[80] good meanes were advised,[81] [*76] whereby Suitors in the *Chancerie*, and such like Courts, might before their day

---

[74] a man] *H;* men *F BT.*

[75] learned in] *F BT;* deeply grounded in the learninge of *H.*

[76] Common Lawes of this Realme] *F BT* (*BT reads* the Realme); Common lawe *H.*

[77] accomplished] *F BT;* thoroughly accomplished *H.*

[78] for Equity] *H;* of (Equity) *F;* and Equitie *BT. There follows here in H (and very similarly in BT):* And hath sent Buishopps (as Kinge Edward the third once did) to their benefices againe as men meeter for Churches then for Courts and soe more properly to be holden in their owne standings then to be permitted to followe the factions of other men.

[79] *This and the following paragraph are omitted in H.*

[80] some] *F;* that some *BT.*

[81] advised] *F;* devised *BT.*

of hearing, which they purchase not without great expences[82] learne whether they shall be dismissed thence to the tryall of the *Common Lawes*, or no; which thing whether it might be better performed by suffering *Plea*, to the Jurisdiction of the Court, or by summary consideration of the case, collected out of the Bill and answer, or by a faithfull report of the estate of the matter, under the *Oath*, and at the perill of both parties; or by some other way, I will leave to the Iudgement of such as have more *Wisedome* to advise,[83] and *Power* to execute.

Againe, when as the *Chancerie*, or any such Court shall be intituled to hold *Plea* of right of Land upon the[84] suggestion of uncertaine *Charters* or *Evidences*[85] should be brought [*77] into the Court; that the parties should be dismissed to the *Common Law*, or[86] enterplead for the[87] *Right* in the *Land;* that those *Evidences* also should be sent thither at the day of *Tryall*, to be given in *Evidence;* and that, according to the *Right*, should[88] fall out for the *Land:* So the *Charters* also should be delivered to the one, or to the other of the parties: Whereas now it is often seene, that one man doth implead another, by this pretence, in the Court of *Equitie*, for cause that requireth no helpe of *Equitie* at all; but doth most properly pertaine to the determinations of the *Common Law.*

But[89] leaving to others the consideration of this also; let mee summe up the rest of your[90] *Lay Courts*, and labour to make[91] an end of them.

---

82 expences] *F;* laboure and expences *BT.*

83 advise] *F;* devise *BT.*

84 the] *F;* a *BT.*

85 Charters or Evidences] *F;* Chartres (or evidences) the whiche the defendent confessethe himselfe to have, but withall mainteynethe the withholding of them for preservation of his owne interest, I cowld wishe, that it might bee ordered, that theise Chartres (or Evidences) *BT.*

86 or] *F;* to *BT.*

87 the] *F;* their *BT.*

88 to the Right, should] *F;* as the right should *BT.*

89 But] *F BT;* I have stayed longe in Chancery, and therefore *H* (*which lacks the two preceding paragraphs*).

90 your] *F;* our *H BT.*

91 and labour to make] *F;* and make *BT;* that I may drawe to *H.*

[*78] THE COURT OF STAR-CHAMBER.

As in the Government of all *Common-weales*, sundry things doe fall out, both in *Peace* and *Warre*, that doe require an extraordinarie helpe, and cannot await the usuall cure of common *Rule*, and setled *Iustice;* the which is not performed, but altogether after one sort, and that not without delay of helpe, and dispense of time: So, albeit here within this Realme of *England*, the most part of *Causes* in complaint are and ought to be referred to the ordinarie processe & solemne handling of *Common Law*, and regular distribution of *Iustice;* yet have there alwayes arisen, and there will continually, from time to time, grow some rare matters, meet (for just reason) to be reserved to a higher hand, and to be left to the aide of [*79] absolute *Power*, and irregular *Authoritie*.

The three parts of this Discourse.

The which thing that it may the more plainely appeare by particularitie, it shall peradventure be worthy the labour to examine: First, for what sort of *Offences* the[92] *Suits* ought to be commenced; then, before *whom* they ought to be heard; and lastly, what speciall *Place* hath beene the most usuall and frequented Court, for the receiving of the same.

THE FIRST PART OF THIS DISCOURSE.[93]

Seeing that all *Actions* be eyther *Civill*, or *Criminall*, that is, either concerning *Right*, or *Revenge;* and the *Common Place* heareth the *Suits* of *Civill nature*, and the *Kings Bench* receiveth those things[94] that doe concerne *Offences:* [*80] It might seeme that all manner of *Suits* (both *Common*, and of the *Crowne*) ought to be drawne in the[95] one or the other of

---

[92] the] *F;* those *H WF.*
[93] Discourse] *F;* Treatise *H WF.*
[94] things] *F; om. H WF.*
[95] in the] *F;* into *H;* into the *WF.*

the[96] Courts; and that it should be in vaine to imagine upon any other *Iudgement-place* besides them.

But yet, even as by the usage of all *Lawes* it is confessed, that in the necessitie of *Civill Causes,* and calamities of that kind, recourse may be had to the *Praetor,* or *Chancellor,* for aid against the inflexible *rigour* of the *Common Law:* So likewise it is to be granted, that wheresoever the ordinarie Courts of *Iustice* be hindered in their course and orderly proceeding; or where the *Evill* and *Crime* it selfe is either new in *Device,* for which no *Law* hath beene yet provided; or where the *Mischiefe* doth surmount the common growth so farre, that standing *Law* hath no reach, nor condigne punishment, [*81] to make it exemplarie; there, and in such cases, *helpe* and *supply* must elsewhere be sought, and found; or otherwise, *Iustice* must limpe on the better legge, and must let *Offenders* to escape, and passe unpunished.

Now, albeit these *Offences* be variable, and infinite in their sundry sorts, according to the changeable and bottomelesse *Devices* and *Draughts* of those wicked *Artificers,* out of whose *Shops* they be sent; so as I may truly say with the Poet,

Non mihi si linguae centum, sint oraque centum,
Ferrea vox, omnes scelerum comprehendere formas,
Omnia poenarum percurrere nomina possem.

Yet, to the end that they may in some open manner be detected, I will endeavour to containe them all within some of these generall bounds that doe ensue.

[*82] THE SUNDRY SORTS OF EXTRAORDINARIE CRIMINALL CAUSES.

As all these extraordinarie *Causes* be in their owne nature *Criminall,* and not *Civill;* so all these *Criminall* doe proceed

---

[96] the] *F;* these *H WF.*

either from *Fraud*, or *Force*, or from them both mixed together; and likewise they be all committed either by publike or private persons, and sometimes against the one and other, sometimes against the other of them.

THE OFFENCES OF PUBLIKE PERSONS.[97]

By the misdemeanours of publike men, and *Officers*, that are forged out of *fraud*, and *wilinesse;*[98] I meane the *Corruptions* of the *Iudges* of any Courts, of the *Iustices* of *Peace*, and whatsoever other *Commissioners*, [*83] or *Delegates*, that either for *Covetousnesse* in themselves, or through *Friendship*, or *Hatred* towards any of the parties, will dip their owne fingers in the *Suits* that depend before them; and will be seene more like to affectionate *Advocates*, or *Parties*, than to sincere and indifferent *Iudges;* either racking *Law* too long, that it may overreach the one side; or shrinking it too short, that the benefit thereof shall not extend to the other side; or otherwise, indirectly abusing the *course* of their Courts, or leaping the Pale of *integritie*, and *Iustice;* within the limits or[99] bounds whereof, they ought to have[1] and keepe them. And in this part, as some may slyly abuse those good gifts, in respect of which they are called to the *Magistracie;* so other-some sticke not to use meanes both forcible and subtill, for the winning of their wills: [*84] thinking, that for their apparant *Nobilitie*, ancient *Gentrie*, large *Possessions*, overflowing *Riches*, or store of *Friends*, (joyned with the *Roomes* of high *Authoritie*, that they have above their *Neighbours*) no passage ought to bee fore-closed against them; howsoever it lead both to the discredit of themselves, and to the danger or undoing of other men.

Now, howsoever there be no ordinarie *Medicine* of *Lawes*

---

[97] The Offences of publike persons] *F WF; om. H.*

[98] and wilinesse] *H WF; om. F.*

[99] limits or] *F; om. H WF.*

[1] have] *F;* hold *H WF.*

for infinite particular *Maladies*, that be caused of these evill *humours;* yet I doubt not, but that all *wise Men* will readily acknowledge, that there is not any one kind of *Example*, proceeding from any Court of ordinarie resort, that can be more fruitfull or beneficiall to the *Common good*, than it shall be by some stately *Authoritie*, to checke the *insolencies* and *outrages* (if any such shall happen) [*85] of the[2] *Iudges, Iustices*, and other men that be great by their places, and *Authoritie;* for thereby both themselves may be either amended, or removed; their equalls shall be taught to beware, to take[3] heed, and their inferiours shall quake for feare, when seeing their betters condignely punished, they can promise to themselves no hope of escape, or impunitie.

THE MISDEMEANORS OF PRIVATE MEN.

On the other side, the private and meaner sort of men, wanting the furniture of *Authoritie*, and of sundry other Advantages, wherewith the great[4] ones are apparelled, doe beat their braines for the finding out of shifts and subtilities, and doe for the most part lay Hookes, and make Traps as it were for the [*86] taking, intangling, and snaring of silly and simple folks.

And hereof spring those so many cunning Cosenages, crafty reaches, undermining devices, subtile complots, counterfeit drifts, and fraudulent fetches; the Egges whereof be laid sometimes by desire of money, and sometime by thirst of revenge, but be alwayes, or for the most part[5] hatched by *Perjurie, Briberie*, and *Corruption*, and are wholly addressed to the discredit of the good name of some, to the detriment of others in their Goods and Fortunes, and to the great danger, and hazard of the bodie and life of many a man.

And here againe it is not meet and just, that when the

---

[2] the] *F;* these *H WF.*

[3] beware, to take] *F;* beware and take *H WF.*

[4] great] *F;* greater *H WF.*

[5] or for the most part] *F;* or for the more parte *WF; om. H.*

wicked sort of men have excogitated any thing with great Labour of wit and cunning, so as it may seeme they have drawne a quintessence of mischiefe, [*87] and set the same abroach, to the remedilesse hurt of the good and quiet Subject; Is it not meet[6] (I say) that Authoritie it selfe also, which is the ordinance of *God*, for the defence of the one, and punishment of the other, should straine the line of *Iustice* beyond the ordinarie length and wonted measure, and thereby take exquisite avengement upon them for it? yea is it not right necessarie, that the most *godly*, *honourable*, *wise*, and *learned* persons of the Land, should be appealed unto, that they may apply new remedies for these new diseases, and that they may be prayed to whet, and exercise the edge of their honourable Authorities, excellent Wisdomes, and gifts of the highest learning against such divellish imposters, mischievous deceivers, and most dangerous *Sycophants?* No lesse reason it is also, [*88] that all such good and upright *Iustices*, *Commissioners*, *Officers*, and whatsoever publike persons, as without seeking any by-paths, or starting holes, doe walke *Regia via* in their severall duties, (and yet neverthelesse be assailed by the evill tongues, oppugned by the injurious wrenches, or discomforted by the unruly countenances of insolent men) should have some place whereunto, in default of common helpe, they may flye for refuge, as to a certaine *Sanctuarie*, and *holy Anchor*, and where they may shrowd themselves in their innocencie, and finde the defence of their Authoritie at the hands of them, by whose gift, meanes, or commendation they first received the same.

[*89] THE[7] APPARANT LACKE OF ORDINARIE HELPE.[7]

But lest it be said unto me, that these things be not hid from the *Wisdome* of the standing *Law*, which hath also opened remedie by way of ordinarie jurisdiction in whatsoever evills

---

[6] meet] meet and just *F H WF*.

[7] The . . . Helpe] *F; om. H;* The Want of Ordinarie helpe *WF*.

of these kindes, it shall be meet for the more manifestation of that which I intend, to fall to some more specially, and to exemplifie my whole conceit, by giving a true taste of all in these few heads of particular cases.

1 If therefore such a one as hath *Iura regalia,* will denie originall *Writs,* or other meanes of *Iustice.*

2 If one that hath a judiciall place, shall by corruption mislead the whole course of an *Evidence* given to a *Iurie* that is charged before him, or shall pleasingly heare [*90] the proofes of the one partie, and peremptorily cut off the other, whereby the truth of their controversie is not brought to light.

3 If a good and serviceable *Iudge, Iustice,* or *Officer* shall bee baited, and bitten with libells and slanders that be not actionable.

4 If a *Iustice* of peace shall bee contemptuously despised, and offered indignities, for which no private Action will bee maintained.

5 If one shall attempt to coyne monie, and shall be deprehended in the doing thereof before he hath performed it.

6 If a Counseller at the Law shall give advice standing with the Learning at *Law,*[8] and yet tending onely to vexation, delay of *Iustice,* or deceit of private persons, or to the defrauding of the Queenes Majestie in her lawfull *Prerogative,* or [*91] to the breaking of a good and wholesome *Statute-Law.*

7 If a man of behaviour and countenance, shall secretly practice with others for the beating or murthering of any other person, and bringeth it not to effect.

8 If Cities, Townships, Colledges, or other Corporations, shall wilfully wrangle, and factiously rent themselves in sunder, whereby their whole politique body shall be hindered, or otherwise become unprofitable; or shall causelesly discountenance, or displace any honest person of their company.

---

[8] at Law] *F;* of the lawe *H WF.*

9 If one private member of such a body, shall by vexation in *Law* so unquiet the Head, and all the rest of the Companie, that they cannot apply their common calling.

10 If Wilfull *perjurie* be committed by any person, in case where no *Indictment* lyeth, nor *Action* upon [*92] the *Statute* of *Perjurie* may be maintained.

11 If a man should accuse another to the Queenes *Majestie*, for speaking words against her, and cannot maintaine the accusation.

12 If a man shall wilfully offend a *Proclamation* made by her *Majestie* upon urgent cause, for a time onely, and untill that *Law* by *Parliament* may be provided.

13 If the *Iurie*, or *Homage* in a *Court Baron*, will passe against plaine *Evidence*, in a *Plaint* of *Aiel Formedone*, or such like.

14 If a *Grand Iurie* will, against their *Evidence*, finde *Ignoramus;* or a *Iurie* for *Life*, or *Death*, will finde a hainous *murtherer* to be *Not guiltie*.

15 If an *Officer* that ought to be sworne, will exercise his *Office*, without any[9] *Oath* taken by him.

16 If a lewd fellow shall counterfeit, upon a *Writ* of *Covenant*, [*93] the *Officers Hands*, to deceive her *Maiestie* of her due *Fine;* or the *Hand* of her *Atturney Generall*, for the better passing of a *Pardon;* or shall set the Name of a *Counsellor* to a *Bill* in *Chancerie*, without his privitie and knowledge.

17 If one that is sued upon a *Title* of *Lease*[10] for yeeres, be *outlawed*, and hath his *Pardon*, and yet will conceale his *Pardon*, and cause his *Chattels* to be seized for the Queene, and then procure them to be committed to a friend of his.

18 If[11] a man will suborne some to appeare for others as *Defendants*, in a *Criminall Cause*.[11]

---

[9] any] *F;* such *H WF.*
[10] Lease] *F;* a Lease *H WF.*
[11] 18 If . . . Cause] *H WF; om. F (which therefore numbers the next item* 18).

19 If a coozening Crew shall entice a young man to the companie of a woman, and cause him to be deprehended by one that pretendeth to be her Husband; and so, for his redemption, he sealeth Leases of his Lands, and maketh Gifts[12] [*94] of his Goods: If (I say) any of these, or the like misdemeanours, (whereof the number is infinite) shall be committed, I see not how they may be chastised by the Rod of any ordinarie *Authoritie*, standing *Law*, or *Statute*.

And therefore, considering that they tend (though in divers degrees) to the dishonour of *God*, the contempt of her Royall *Majestie*, the disturbance of the *Common peace*, and the disherison, danger, & death of good *Subjects;* I suppose, that no man will be either so wicked, as to affirme, that they ought not to be punished; or so unadvised, as to hold, that the ancient and godly *Policie* of this *Kingdome*, and *Commonwealth*, hath not left the meanes to bring them into *Iudgement:* For howsoever the *Nationall*, *Civill*, or *Positive Lawes* of particular People and Countries (which doe worke [*95] upon *Generalities*, and must therefore faile in many *Specialls*) doe not provide *punishment* for all sorts of *evils* that may arise; yet may it not be doubted, but that the *Iustice* of *God* (whereof the *Law* of *Humanitie*, *Reason*, and *Nature* hath some remnants saved for us, from that great shipwracke of our first Parent *Adam*) doth keepe[13] correction in store for them.[13]

And therefore let us rather enquire, who it is that both may and ought to award this correction and chastisement for the same.

The Second[14] Part: Enquiring who is Iudge of these extraordinarie Criminalls.[14]

I shall not need to repeat that which I have before this time

---

[12] Gifts] *F;* guift *H WF.*

[13] doth keepe . . . them] *F WF; om. H.*

[14] The Second . . . Criminalls] *F; om. H. F places it before the preceding sentence, and WF has there an equivalent:* The .2. parte: Whoe is the Judge in Extraordinarie causes.

opened, touching the beginning of the Kingly *Power*, and *Authoritie*, [*96] for the deliverie of *Iustice* to all the sorts, and in all the Suits of his Subjects.

The *King*.[15]

But I will confirme by proofs drawn out of our Countrie *Lawes*, and *Lawyers*, that the selfe-same general *jurisdiction* is appropriated to all the *Kings* of this Realme of *England*.

Master *Henry Bracton*, that lived in the time of King *Henry* the third, hath in the *ninth* and *tenth Chapter* of his[16] Booke, these words following: *Rex (& non*[17] *alius) debet judicare, si solus ad id sufficere possit: cum ad hoc per veritatem*[18] *sacramenti teneatur astrictus. Exercere igitur debet Rex*[17] *potestatem Iuris, sicut Dei Vicarius, & Minister in terra. Sin Dominus Rex ad singulas causas determinandas non sufficiat, ut levior sit illi labor in plures personas, partito onere eligere debet viros sapientes, & timentes Deum, & ex illis constituere Iusticiarios.*

The words doe prove two things [*97] serviceable for this purpose: First, That the King ought onely to be the *Iudge* of his people, (if he alone were able to performe that *Office*) as well because hee is within his owne *Kingdome* the *Vice-roy* of *God*, (the supreme *Iudge* of the World) as also for that hee is thereunto bounden by *Oath*, taken at the[19] *Coronation*. The second, That albeit he doe (for the multitude of *Causes*) substitute others underneath him, yet is hee not thereby discharged himselfe; for it is done, *ut levior sit illi labor*, that his labour be the lighter; not, that he should sit unoccupied. And lest you should doubt, that so much is not comprised in that *Oath* of his, one *question* therein, amongst others, is this; *Facies*

---

15 The King] *F WF; om. H.*

16 Chapter of his] *F;* Chapters of his *H;* chapters of his .3. booke *WF.*

17 Rex (& non . . . Rex] *H WF;* Rex *F.*

18 veritatem] *F;* virtutem *H WF.*

19 the] *F;* his *H WF.*

fieri in omnibus Iudiciis tuis aequam, & rectam Iustitiam, & discretionem in misericordia & veritate secundum vires tuas: To the which hee answereth, [*98] *faciam:* wherein the words *Iudiciis tuis, & vires tuas*, doe more properly denote his owne doing, than the doing of his subalterne *Iustices;* albeit their *Iudgement* be after a certaine manner, the *Iudgement* of the King himselfe also, from whence their *Authoritie* is derived.

Much like the words of *Bracton*, speaketh King *Edward* the first, in the beginning of his Book of *Lawes*, commonly called *Brittan:* where, after hee had[20] shewed that hee is the *Vicar* of *God*, and that he hath distributed his *Charge* into sundry portions, because he alone is not sufficient to heare and determine all complaints of his people; then he addeth these words: *Nous volons que nostre Iurisdiction soit sur touts Iurisdictions en nostre Realme: Issint que en touts maners de Felonies, Trespas, Contracts, & en touts maners de autres actions personals, ou real ayons poer a rendre,* [*99] *& faire rendre les Iudgments tiels come ils afferont sans auter processe, par la ou nous scavons la droit verite come Iuges:* Wee will (saith the King) that our owne *Iurisdiction* be above all the *Iurisdiction* of our *Realme:* So as in all manner of *Felonies, Trespasses, Contracts,* and in all[21] other *Actions personalls* or *Realls*, we have *power* to yeeld (or cause to yeeld) such *Iudgements* as doe appertaine (without other *Processe*) wheresoever wee know the right truth, as *Iudges.*

Neither may this be taken to be meant of the *Kings Bench*, where there is only an imaginarie presence of his *Person;* but it must necessarily be understood of a *Iurisdiction* remaining, and left in the *Kings* Royall *Body* and *Brest*, distinct from that of his *Bench, Marshalsey, Common Pleas, Exchequer*, and the

---

[20] after hee had] *F;* after that he hath *H WF.*

[21] all] *F;* all manner of *H WF.*

other ordinarie Courts: because he doth immediately after, in the same place, severally [*100] set forth by themselves, as well the *Authoritie* of the *Kings Bench*, as of the rest of those his ordinarie Courts of *Iustice*.

And that this was no new-made *Law*, or first brought in by the *Norman Conquest*, I must put you in mind of that which I have vouched before, out of the *Saxon Lawes* of King *Edgar*, where you did reade it thus: *Nemo in lite Regem appellato, nisi quando*[22] *domi jus consequi non poterit, sin juris summi onere domi prematur, ad Regem ut is id oneris allevet, provocato:* Let no man in *Suit* appeale to the King, unlesse he may not get *right* at home; but if that *right* be too heavie for him, goe[23] to the King to have it eased. By which it may evidently appeare, that even so many yeeres[24] agoe there might *Appellation* be made to the Kings *Person*, whensoever the *Cause*[25] should enforce it.

[*101] THE KINGS COUNCELL.[26]

But now although I speake here expressely of the *Kings* person, yet I meane not so precisely, as though that either the *King* ought to performe these Iudgements in his owne person alone, or that hee must of necessitie be present in person, whensoever others shall accomplish them on his behalfe.

Only I doe affirme, that the *King* hath a supreme Court of *Prerogative*, whereunto his Subjects in such their necessities may provoke, as to his owne *Royall person;* and wherein there is place left for him to sit, the which our *Kings* in person have oftentimes frequented, and were assisted with such men of *Nobilitie*, *Wisedome*, and *Learning*, as he shall chuse, he may

---

[22] quando] *F;* quidem *H WF.*

[23] goe] *F;* then lett him goe *H WF.*

[24] many yeeres] many hundred yeeres *F H WF.*

[25] Cause] *H WF;* King's Cause *F.*

[26] The Kings Councell] *F WF; om. H.*

in *Royall presence* use his judiciall *Authoritie*, or[27] otherwise [*102] for the time abstaine to be *present* there, and leave the proceedings to those selected men: but yet so, as both the *suits* bee exhibited to *himselfe* by *name*, and that he also receive *intelligence* thereof when as it shall be requisite: and these men thus taken for their *counsell* and *advice*, wee doe commonly call *The Kings Councell;* which *words* forasmuch as it is diversly used in our Law, and doth not alwayes import the same thing, it shall be fit in some few words to distinguish the significations, and sorts thereof.

The generall Assembly in *Parliament*, is termed in our old *Writs*, *Commune Consilium Regni Angliae*, the Common Councell of the Realme of *England*, called together by the *King*, for advice in matters concerning the whole Realme: of which Assemblie, some be *Counsellors* by [*103] Birth, as the *Barons;* some by Succession, as the *Bishops;* and some by Election, as *Knights* and *Burghesses;* and these be all (for the time) the *Kings Councell. The Masters* of the *Requests* also, which doe hold Plea of *Complaints* exhibited for *Equitie* to his owne person, be according to the usuall forme of writing there, named the *Kings Councell.*

And besides both these, there is another *Councell* of the *King*, whereof there is mention made by name both in the Statute 37. *Edward* 3. *cap.* 18. which I reserve to be hereafter recited for another purpose, and likewise in one agreement of an Exchange, had for the Castle of *Berwicke*, betweene King *Henry* the fourth, in the 5. yeere of his Reigne, and the Earle of *Northumberland*, where the King promiseth to deliver to the Earle, Lands and Tenements to the value of the Castle, [*104] by these words, *Per avise & assent des Estates de son Roymalme, & de son Parlement (perainsi que Parlement soit devant le Feast de St.* Lucie) *ou auterment per assent de son*

---

[27] or] or may *F H WF.*

grand Counseil, & auters Estates de son dit Realme, que le Roy ferra assembler devant le dit Feast en case que le Parlement ne soit, &c. That is;[28] By the advice and assent of the Estates of his Realme, and of his Parliament, (so that the Parliament happen before the Feast of St. *Lucie;*) otherwise, by the assent of his *Great Councell*, and other Estates of his said Realme, which the King will cause to bee assembled before the said Feast, in case the Parliament doe not happen, &c. as in the instrument thereof, Dated at *Lichfield* 27. of *August*, in that yeere, and remaining in the *Tower*, may be read.

By which words it is plaine, that there is a *Great Councell* besides the [*105] *Parliament*, which no doubt, is the same whereof the *Statute* (made afterwards in the 13. yeere of the same King *Henry* 4. *chap.* 7. against *Riots*, doth specially speake, commanding, that where the truth of a *Riot* may not be found by the inquirie of twelve men,[29] there the *Iustices* of the *peace*, and *Sheriffe*, or *Under-Sheriffe* shall certifie before the King and his Councell all the deeds and circumstances thereof: which speech cannot be meant, either of the *Chancerie*, or of the *Kings Bench*, because the latter is distinguished from it by expresse words of the same Statute, and the former was afterward 8. *Hen.* 6. *cap.* 14. enabled to receive Certificats of this kinde, by the letters of the same *Iustices* and *Sheriffe* or *Under-sheriffe*.

This *Councell* of the *King*, consisteth onely of persons thereunto especially elected by *himselfe*, and [*106] thereupon sworne to serve him with their faithfull advice and counsell; and whether they be *Nobles*, or no, it is not materiall, seeing that the Calling commeth not by *Birth*, but groweth by *Election;* so as[30] it excludeth all that be not admitted: A thing that

---

[28] That is;] *H WF;* And this *F.*
[29] men] *F; om. H WF.*
[30] so as] *F WF;* so that *H.*

may well appeare, not onely by the speciall forme of their *Oath*, by the number of themselves (distinctly knowne to bee more or lesse at sundry times) by keeping in Record the entrie of their severall *Names*, and by the *Fee* that each of them doth ratably pay after his degree when he is admitted: but also by experience of former times, and not without some example of Execution in our owne Age: And they also of this *Councell* of the *King*, have bin diversly termed some[31] of the *Privie Councell*, for that they were[31] more inwardly and secretly used in matters of Estate: Besides, that [*107] they were ordinarily imployed also upon other causes with the rest that have beene called of[32] Councell at large.

For whereas it is reported in *Dorso clauso de Anno* 16. *Edwar.* 2. *Membr.* 5. That *Henry* the Lord *Beaumont* was for his unreverent speeches to the *King*, commanded out of the *Councell-house*, it is there said withall, that he was *Iuratus de magno & secreto Consilio Regis;* howbeit they both are for this our purpose, that great *Councell* of the *King* whereof I spake even now, and be so incorporate with him, as hee speaketh by them, and their *Iudgements* are reputed to bee his owne: To[33] which I may the more boldly affirme, when I read 2. *Rich.* 3. 11. & 18. *Hen.* 8. 1. That *Fynes* assessed by the *Kings Iustices* of any *Court*, are to be understood to bee *Fynes* adjudged by the *King himselfe.* [*108] And thus now[34] have I both *shewed* and *confirmed* who it is that ought to hearken to these *complaints.*

THE CONFLICTS BETWEENE THE LAW ABSOLUTE AND ORDINARIE.

But here have I mightie Adversaries to encounter withall; the which maintaining with their whole Forces the ordinarie

[31] some . . . they were] *H WF; om. F.*

[32] of] *F;* of the *H WF.*

[33] To] *F;* The *H WF.*

[34] now] *H WF; om. F.*

Iurisdiction, will in no wise yeeld to any such absolute and unbridled *Authoritie*, as I may seeme to advance.

And therefore first of all, that *Great Charter* of the *Liberties* of *England*, (which I may call the first *Letters* of *Manumission* of the people of this *Realme* out of the *Norman* servitude) doth by the *Mouth* of the King (amongst many other Freedomes) specifie this one: *Nullus liber homo capiatur, vel imprisonetur, aut disseisietur de libero tenemento suo,* [*109] *vel libertatibus, vel liberis consuetudinibus suis, aut utlagetur, ut*[35] *exuletur, aut aliquo modo destruatur, nec super eum ibimus, nec super eum mittemus, nisi per legale judicium parium suorum, vel per Legem terrae.*

By pretence of which *Grant*, the common *Subject* thought himselfe free[36] from that irregular *Power* which the former Kings and their Councell of Estate had exercised upon him; and phantasied, that he ought not thenceforth to be drawne to answer in any *Case*, except it were by way of *Indictment*, or by tryall of good and lawfull men (being his Peeres) onely after the course of the *Common Law:* Whereas indeed, these words of the Statute ought to be understood of the restitution then made of the ordinarie *Iurisdiction* in common *Controversies*, and not for restraint of the absolute *Authoritie;* serving[37] onely in a few rare and [*110] singular *Cases:* And therefore see what followed; some *Cases* dayly creeping out of *Suits*, for which no *Law* had beene provided; and some *misdemeanours* also happening from time to time, in the distribution of those *Lawes* that were alreadie established.

It came to passe, that many finding none other helpes for their griefes, were enforced to sue to the Kings *Person* it selfe, for remedie: And hee againe knowing himselfe to be the *Chiefe Iustice* and *Lieutenant* of *God* within his owne *Realme*,

---

[35] ut] *F;* aut *H WF.*
[36] free] *F;* freed *H WF.*
[37] serving] *F WF;* savinge *H.*

thought himselfe bound to deliver *Iudgement* and *Iustice*, whensoever it should be required at his hands. The which, for as much as he could not evenly, and with uprightnesse performe, unlesse hee called the adversarie partie; neither had he many times, especially in a new and sudden occurrent, any ordinarie *Writ*, or [*111] *Processe*, whereby to call him of necessitie;[38] hee was to resort to the[39] Kingly and absolute *Power* againe, and by his *Pursuivant*, or *Letters*, to convent him, and then to proceed to the hearing and determining of the *Cause*, as to his Princely *Office* did appertaine.

The which thing was so farre from offending the *Subject* for a long time together, that in the *Parliament* 28. *Edw.* 1. *cap.* 5. the *Commons* assented to an Act, by which it was provided, That the *Chancellor* and the *Iustices* of the *Kings Bench* should follow the King wheresoever hee went; to the end, that he might alwaies have at hand men learned, and able to advise him in such *Cases* as he admitted to his hearing.

Neverthelesse, (such is the weaknesse and imperfection of man) the time was not long, but the *Subject*, which so desirously fled to the King [*112] and his Councell for succour, did as hastily retire, and run backe to the ordinarie *Seat* and *Iudge* againe.

The which thing, whether it happened by the chargeable and hard accesse to the person of the King; (who could not but be many wayes busied with more important matters) or by some delay of *Iustice* that fell in his absence out of the *Realme*, by occasion of forraine *Warres*, and other *Affaires*; or by the undertaking of *Causes*, without the advice and presence of the said *Councellors*[40] and *Iustices*, it needeth not any long and curious inquisition: But this is certaine, that within five yeeres next after the beginning of the Reigne of King

---

[38] *H WF place the punctuation before rather than after* of necessitie.

[39] the] *F;* his *H WF.*

[40] Councellors] *F;* Chancellor *H WF.*

Edward the third, it was commanded by *Parliament*, That the forme of the *Great Charter*, in this point, should be wholly and inviolably observed. And for the more assured suppression [*113] of all attempts that might breake forth to the contrarie, it was afterwards by the *Parliaments*, 25. *Edward*. 4.[41] *cap*. 4. 28. *Edward*. 3. *cap*. 31. provided and prohibited, That no man should be put to answere before the King, or his Councell, without presentment before the *Iustices*, due *Processe*, matter of *Record*, and[42] *Writ* originall, according to the ancient *Lawes* of the Land.

Moreover, for the utter discouragement and beating downe of all such as used to preferre unto the King any *Accusations*, *Suggestions*, or *Petitions* against other men, further *Law* was given by the *Parliament*, 37. *Edw*. 3. *cap*. 18. That they should be sent with their *Suggestions*, before the *Chancellor*, *Treasurer*, and the Kings *Great Councell*, and should there put in *Sureties* of *Taliation;* that is, to incurre the same [*114] paine that the other should have, in case the *Suggestion* were found untrue. But one yeeres experience made that Point to be mollified, by the making of a new *Law*, 38. *Edward*. 3. *cap*. 9. which taking away the *Taliation*, gave order, That such false *Suggestors* should be imprisoned onely, untill they had both made full agreement with the partie molested, and *Fine* and *Ransome* with the King.

And then, within a few yeeres after, also these accusations grew still more and more odious: So that it was decreed by the *Parliament*, 42. *Edw*. 3. *cap*. 3. That if any thing should be done in that behalfe contrarie to the old *Law* of the Land, the same should be void in the *Law*, and holden for errour.

Nevertheless, these *Complaints* were yet againe afterwards thought [*115] meet to be admitted: And thereupon the *Statute*, 17. *Rich*. 2. *cap*. 6. willed, the[43] *Chancellor* alone

---

[41] Edward. 4.] *F;* E. 3. *H WF.*
[42] and] *F;* or *H WF.*
[43] the] *F;* that the *H WF.*

should have power, by his discretion, to award Damages against any person that should make untrue suggestion against another, before the Kings Councell: The which Authoritie the *Chancellor* exercised many yeeres together, and until at the length his *Writs* of *Subpoena* flew so thicke abroad, for matters determinable at the *Common Law*, that he also was charged to exceed[44] the bounds of Authoritie delivered unto him: So that the *Parliament*, 15. *Hen.* 6. *cap.* 4. stayed the granting of the *Subpoena*, untill that Suretie were found, to answer to the partie grieved as well his Damages as expences, if that the matter could not be made good, that was contained in the Bill of Complaint against him.

[*116] Now by the tossing of this[45] Ball to and fro, betweene the *Councell* and *Commons*, it may at once very well appeare on the one side how hard, and rare a thing it is, for great men arrayed with high Authoritie, to containe themselves within[46] prefixed limits and pale of their power, and on the other side, how impatient the *Common Man* of this Realme hath alwayes beene, and without doubt yet[47] is, and ever will be, to have his Causes determined either at the *Councell-board* without open hearing, or by absolute authoritie, without prescribed rule of ordinary proceeding; in either of which cases he is very jealous of evill weight, and hard measure[48] in the former, because hee is perswaded, that as his *controversie* is not at the first drawne from the ordinarie tryall without the speciall labour of his *Adversarie*, and for great favour [*117] extended to him: so hee feareth, that the same *good-will* being once planted, will continually possesse the roome, and will prove prejudiciall for him even to the end of his Suit and

---

[44] to exceed] *WF;* not to exceede *F H.*

[45] the tossing of this] *F;* this tossing of the *H WF.*

[46] within] within the *F H WF.*

[47] yet] *F WF;* it *H.*

[48] *H WF end the sentence here with a colon.*

businesse in the latter:[49] because, when he is to be judged by an irregular and uncontroulable *authoritie*, he findeth himselfe utterly destitute of all *counsel* which way to turne him, since no man of *learning* can assure him before-hand what will be the *consciences* or *discretion* of the[50] *Iudges:* whereas the successe may easily be fore-told in most of these other *Controversies* which come to *determination* by *ruled Law* and *bounded jurisdiction.*

The Office of the King.[51]

It is the Office of the King, to deliver *Iustice.*

And thus whilest the *King* and his *Councell* embraced all manner of Complaints without exception, [*118] the Subjects were thereby many times injuriously vexed, and put to travaile and charge: So as this repugnancie tooke root betweene them, and this *Antinomia* (or *Contrarietie* of *Law*) did spring out of the same: The which howsoever in appearance it may seeme great and irreconciliable, yet if recourse may be had to that *golden Mediocritie*, which both *Religion*, *Reason*, and *Law* doe maintaine in this point, the Controversie will soon be decided, and that without any derogating from the *Authoritie* of the *King* and his *Councell;* or prejudicating that lawfull *Freedome* of the Subject, which is claimed for him. For as it is inseparably annexed to the *Office* of a King, to be the *Iudge* of his people, and as he cannot any longer remaine *King* indeed, than he shall be readie to deliver *Iudgement* and *Iustice* unto them,(†) which two things [*119] *Bracton* saith, *Faciunt ipsam Coronam, nec ab ea separari possunt:* So howsoever

(†) *Casus in* 3. *Polic.* 300. *Cic.* 1. *de Orat.*

---

[49] *H WF place the punctuation before* In the latter, *which opens the second of the two cases discussed.*

[50] the] *F;* his *H WF.*

[51] The Office of the King] *om. F H WF (that is, as separate from the marginal heading, which serves in all as the section heading).*

many Courts of ordinarie resort shall bee established by him, yet if either they have not, as I said, *authoritie* to apply Remedie for all wrongs and diseases, or if that *power* and *authoritie* which they have, may not enjoy her free course and passage, then must the King either exercise his *pre-eminent* and *royal Iurisdiction*, or else must the injuriously afflicted be deprived of that helpe and remedie, which both the *Ordinance* of *God*, the *Dutie* of a *Kingly Iudge*, and the *common Law* of *Nature* and *Reason* doe afford unto him.

And on the other side againe, it is not to be doubted, but that if the subject were once utterly barred of this accesse to the person of the King in case of such his distresse, he would cry out upon the ordinarie [*120] *Law*, for the *Authoritie* whereof he so eagerly striveth; and would not sticke to lay to the Kings charge, that hee bare the *Sword* in vaine; that he kept not the promise of the *Great Charter; Nulli negabimus aut differemus Iustitiam;* and that hee violated the *Solemne Oath* and *Vow* of his Coronation, *faciam fieri justitiam.*

The true moderation of[52] Iurisdiction absolute.

What is then to be said? Shall the King and his *Councell* open a Court for all sorts of *Pleas* that be determinable by the course of *Common Law?* that were to set[53] an *Anomy*, and to bring disorder, doubt, and incertaintie over all: Shall no helpe at all bee sought for at the hands of the King, when it cannot be found in the *Common Law?* that [*121] were to stop his eares at the crie of the *oppressed*, and would draw wrath and punishment from *Heaven.*

Betweene these two extremes, *Medio tutissimus ibis*, there lieth a meane, that will both uphold the *Majestie* of the King, maintaine the *Authoritie* of the *Common Courts*, and succour the distressed *Client* in his greatest necessitie. The which, to

[52] of] of the *F H WF.*

[53] set] *F;* sett up *H WF.*

deliver it shortly, is this: If the ordinarie *Iurisdiction* of the *Common Court*[54] be not hindred[55] by this infinite authoritie, but onely where either (as I said) they have no *Warrant* to receive the *Plea*, or where the *tenure* of their due proceedings is disturbed; or where the matter is such, as deserveth to be heard upon the *highest Stage;* or the partie such, as is unable to run the wearisome race of solemne *Law & Processe;* or where some other rare, extraordinary, & weighty *consideration* shall promote the same.

[*122] THE MAINTENANCE OF THAT MODERATION.[56]

And this *Mediocritie* is maintainable, not onely by reason of the Kingly and judiciall *Office* (whereof I have oftentimes spoken) but also by the meaning of many *Statutes*, and by the continuall practice of our owne Kings.

For whereas the *Statute* 27. *Edw.* 3. *cap.* 13. did provide, that if any Merchant were robbed at the Sea of his goods,[57] and the same came to the hands of any person within the Realme, the Merchant should bee received, to prove the goods to bee his owne, either by the[58] *Marke*, *Chartre party*, or *Cocket*, or by the testimonie of good Merchants; and thereupon they should be delivered unto him, without any Suit at the *Common Law.*(†) It was construed, that the Remedie in such a [*123] case was to be had at the hands of the King.

And therefore *Richard* the third, in the 2. yeere of his Reigne, sate in person with his *Councell*, and heard the cause of a *Spanish* Merchant, that sued before him upon the same *Statute*, and in the *Statutes*,[59] 13. *Hen.* 4. *cap.* 7. 19.[60] *Henry*

(†) 13. *Ed.* 4. 9.

---

[54] Court] *F;* Courtes *H WF.*

[55] be not hindred] *F WF; om. H.*

[56] that Moderation] this mediocrity *F H WF.*

[57] at the Sea of his goods] *F;* of his goods at the Sea *H WF.*

[58] the] *F;* his *H WF.*

[59] and in the Statutes] and in that Statute *F;* And, in that the Statutes *H WF. H starts this new sentence as a new paragraph.*

[60] 19.] 9. *F H WF.*

7. *cap.* 13. 31. *Hen.* 6. *cap.* 2. and others, doe make[61] mention of the King, and his *Councell:* it is not so to be wrested, as though they then erected any new authoritie, but onely had regard to that which was before.

Againe, in that the Commons of the Realme assented first in the *Parliament*, 28. *Edward* 1. *cap.* 5. that the *Chancellor* and *Chiefe Iustices* should attend the King with their advice upon these Complaints: then in the *Parliament* 37. *Edward* 3. *cap.* 18. that these Petitioners should put in Suerties of *Taliation.* [*124] After that, in the *Parliament* 38. *Edward* 3. *cap.* 9. that they should bee imprisoned till they satisfied the King, and the party of their false suggestions. And lastly, in the *Parliament* 17. *Richard* 2. *cap.* 6. that *damages* onely should be awarded against them.

It is in all these, I say, covertly confessed, that Complaints upon just *Causes* might be moved before the King and his *Councell*, and that the Commons of the *Realme* sought onely to be delivered from *troubles* and *costs* that grew by *unjust accusations:* Which also is made plaine in that Petition of the *Commons* (of *Parliament* 1. *Henry* 6. *Numb.*[62] 41. in the *Records*) where they prayed, That none should be called before the *Chancellor*, or the Kings *Councell*, for any matter, but such onely as had no remedie at the *Common Law;* and in such case also, by the testimonie [*125] of an *Indenture*, to be made betweene the *Plaintifes* and two of the *Iudges* of either *Bench*. And albeit the *Commons* have seemed in some other *Parliaments* generally, and without any exception, to impugne this Kingly *Prerogative;* yet here the Kings alwayes most gravely and considerately repelled that sort of attempt: As, when in the *Parliament* begun at *Glocester*, 2. *Richard*. 2. the *Commons* made a Supplication to the King, That no *Writ*

---

[61] make] use *F H WF.*

[62] Numb.] membr. *F H;* num. *WF.*

out of the *Chancerie*, or *Letter* of *Privie Seale*, might be directed, to make any appeare before the Kings Councell, or others, to answer touching his *Freehold;* but that the *Common Law* of the Land bee maintained, to have her full course: The King then[63] answered, That he thought it not reasonable, that he should be restrained to send for his *Lieges* upon cause unreasonable.[64] [*126] And albeit he did not purpose, that such as were so sent for, should answer *Finalment* peremptorily touching their *Free-hold*, but should be demanded[65] for tryall thereof, as *Law* required it:[66] *Purvie touts voyes que a Suits*[67] *de partie, ou le Roy & son Counceil seroit creablement enformees, que (pur Maintenances, Oppressions, & autres outrages dascun en pais) le Common Ley ne purra avoyer duement son course, que en tiel case le Counceil purra envier pur le person, pur luy metre a response de sa misprision: & a leur bon discretion de luy compeller a faire suertie per serement, & in autre maner de son bon partie,*[68] *& que il ne ferra maintenance ne autre riens que purra disturber le course del Common Ley in*[69] *oppression du people.* Provided alwayes, (saith he) That at the *Suit* of the Partie, where the King and his Councell shall be credibly informed, that (because of *Maintenances*, [*127] *Oppressions*, or other *Outrages* of any persons in the Countrey) the *Common Law* cannot have[70] her course; in such case, the Councell may send for the partie upon whom the *Complaint* is made, to make his answer for his contempt: and furthermore, by their good discretion to compell him to finde *Sureties* by *Oath*, or in other manner, for his good behaviour; and that he shall not by himselfe, or by any other, commit

---

[63] then] *F; om. H WF.*

[64] unreasonable] reasonable *F H WF.*

[65] demanded] *F;* remanded *H WF.*

[66] it] *F; yett (preceded by the colon) H WF.*

[67] Suits] *F;* suite *H WF.*

[68] partie] part *F WF;* porte *H.*

[69] in] *F;* en *H WF.*

[70] have] *F;* have duly *H WF.*

Maintenance, or other thing, which may disturbe the course of the *Common Law*.

And likewise, when as the *Commons* in the *Parliament* holden at *Westminster* in the 13. yeere of the same *King*, did pray, That upon pain of a forfeiture, the *Chancellour* or *Councell* of the *King* should not, after the end of the[71] *Parliament*, make any *Ordinance* against the *Common Law*, or the ancient *Customes* or *Statutes* [*128] of the Land; nor make any *Writ* called *Quibusdam certis de causis*, for the answering in any sort, where *Recoverie* is given by the *Common Law*, but that the *Common Law* should run wholly amongst all the people; and that no *Iudgement* given should be adnulled, without due processe of the *Law*. The King then answered thus: *Soit use come ad estre use devant ses heures issint, que la Regalie du Roy soit sauve; car le Roy voit saver sa Regalie come ses progenitors ont fait devant luy: & si ascun soyent*[72] *grieve, monstre en special, & droit luy serra fait.* Let it be used (saith the King) as it hath beene used before this time, so as the Regalitie of the King be saved; for the King will save his Regalitie, as[73] his Progenitors have done:[73] And if any person doe finde himselfe grieved, let him shew it in specialitie, and right shall be done unto him.

[*129] Moreover, where in the *Parliament* holden the fourth yeere of King *Henry* the fourth, the *Commons* complained, That notwithstanding the said *Statute* 25. *Edw.* 3. *cap.* 3.[74] many of the Kings Liege people were unquieted; some, by Writs of *Subpoena*, issuing upon false suggestions out of the *Chancerie;* some, by that *Writ* out of the *Exchequer*, called *Quia datum est nobis intelligi;* and some, by *Letters* of *Privie Seale:* and therefore prayed the King, That the partie accused might be received, to traverse such surmises, and to

---

[71] the] *F;* that *H WF.*

[72] soyent] soylent *F;* soy sent *H WF.*

[73] as . . . done] *F WF; om. H.*

[74] cap. 3.] *F H;* cap. 4 *WF* (*agrees with citation p. *113*).

trie them by an *Enquest;* which also if they found for him, might give him *Damages*, with regard of his *Slander*, *Costs*, and *Travaile;* and that the *Accuser* should not onely make *Fine* and *Ransome* to the King, but also endure *imprisonment* by the space of a yeere.

[*130] The Kings answer then was, That hee would give in charge to his *Officers*, that they should abstaine more than before-time they had, to send for his *Subjects* in that manner: But yet (saith he) it is not our intention, that our *Officers* shall so abstaine, that they may not send for our *Subjects* in matters and causes necessarie, as it hath beene used in the time of our good[75] Progenitors.

Finally, when as in the *Parliament* 3. *Hen.* 5. the *Commons* eftsoones complaining against those *Writs* of *Subpoena*, and *Quibusdam certis de causis*, and *Quia datum est nobis intelligi*, which issued of[76] matters determinable at the *Common Law*, and that were (as they said) first devised in the time of King *Richard* the second, by the subtletie of *Ioh. Waltham*, the *Bishop* of *Salisbury:* And therefore prayed [*131] the King, that it might be enacted, That those *Writs* should be enrolled in the Courts from whence they proceeded, and thereby made open to the *Defendant*, that hee might thereupon have his *Action* of *Debt* for fortie pounds against him that should pursue any such. The answer was; *Le Roy s'advisera*, The King will be advised of it: The which is the same phrase whereby the Kings of this Realme doe use to denie their assent to any *Act* that hath passed the *Lords* and *Commons* in *Parliament*.

All which *Rescripts* and *Answers* of the Kings, doe fully disclose that *Moderation* which I seeke; that is, That the course of the *Common Law* be commonly holden; That men bee not causelesly convented before the King, and his *Councell;* and

---

[75] good] *H WF; om. F.*

[76] which issued of] *F;* that issued for *H WF.*

that the proceeding at the *Councell-Board*, be not upon every [*132] light suggestion, nor to determine finally concerning *Free-hold*, or *Inheritance*. And yet, that upon cause reasonable, upon credible information, and that in matters necessarie, the Kings *Regalitie*, *Prerogative*, or *Iudiciall Power*, in sending for his *Subjects*, be maintained, as of right it ought, and before[77] hath beene used. The which thing (as you see) is so farre from impeaching the free course of the *Common Law*, that it not onely concurreth with her, and removeth all impediments of her proceeding, where shee hath the *Iurisdiction:* But also, by the plentitude of the Royall *Power*, supplyeth her wants, and defects, wheresoever shee is not authorized to deliver the helpe of *Iustice*.

[*133] EXAMPLES OF THAT MODERATION.[78]

According to this moderation, King *Edward* 1. seeing that *Bogo de Clare* was discharged of an *accusation* put against him in *Parliament;* for some imperfections of forme that were discovered in the *Complaint*, commanded him neverthelesse to appeare before himselfe, *ad faciendum & recipiendum quod per regem & ejus consilium fuerit faciendum*, and so proceed to a[79] reexamination of the whole cause, *Anno* 18. *Edward* 1.

And according to this *Moderation*, King *Edward* 3. in the 41. yeere of his Reigne, at the *complaint* of *Elizabeth*, the widdow of *Nicholas Audley*,[80] to appeare before himselfe[81] and his *Councell*, (*viz.*) the *Chancellor*, *Treasurer*, and *Iustices*, and other *Sages*, and upon their submission [*134] to stand to the ordinance of him, and his *Councell*, he determined a controversie betweene them, touching the assurance of cer-

---

[77] before] *F;* as before tyme *H WF*.

[78] Examples of that Moderation] Examples of Moderation *F; om. H;* Examples of this moderation *WF*.

[79] proceed to a] proceed by *F;* proceeded to a *H WF*.

[80] Audley,] *F;* Audley, commandeth James Audley *H WF*.

[81] himselfe] *F;* him *H WF*.

taine Lands contained in the Covenants of her marriage. *Rot. clauso de Anno.* 41. *Edward* the third.

According to this *Moderation*, King *Henry* 5. in a *Suit* before him and his *Councell*, betweene *William Goddard* and his Wife, *complainants* against *Hugh Straule* for the title of the Mannor of *Serrie*, and St. *Laurence*, in the Isle of *Tannet* in *Kent*, tooke order for sequestring the profits, till the right were tryed; as well for the avoiding of the breach of the peace, as for the prevention of waste and spoile. *Rot. Paten. Anno* 6. *Henry* 6.

According to this *Moderation*, when *Robert Danvers*, a Counsellor at the *Law*, had[82] exhibited his Bill to King *Henry* 6. and his *Councell*, in [*135] the 11. yeere of his Reigne, praying thereby, That forasmuch as he was defamed with the suspicion of raising[83] a *Record*, of an *Inquisition* after the death of *Iohn Saint-Iohn*, the matter might be examined, aswell for the behalfe of the King, as for the declaration of his owne innocencie. The request was granted unto him, and upon proofe, that *William Brocket*, a Clarke of the Exchequer, had made the razure, *Brocket* was fore-judged to have accesse for writing in any of the Kings Courts of *Record*, and *Danvers* was acquitted of all fault; with order, that his[84] *Declaration* of his innocencie should be inrolled.

The like whereof, for the *Declaration* of the innocencie to[85] the Lord *Ralph Cromwell*, *Chamberlaine* to the same King, made by him before the Kings *Councell*, against the villanous accusation of one *Robert Collison*, [*136] Priest, for suspition of Treason, may you read in *Rot. Paten. de Anno* 31. *Henry* 6.

According to the same *Moderation* also, the *Counsell* of the same King proceeded against *Iohn Foard*, a *Mercer* of *Lon-*

---

[82] had] *F; om. H WF.*
[83] raising] *F;* razinge *H WF.*
[84] his] *F;* this *H WF.*
[85] to] *F;* of *H WF.*

don; and punished him for the[86] fraudulent packing of 26. stone of Wooll amongst certaine Broad Cloathes, that he sold to a *Dutchman*, which did transport them; *Rotulo Claus. de Anno* 17. *Henry 6.*

According to this *Moderation*, the same King likewise commanded the *Iustices* of his *Bench* to stay the *arraignment* of one *Verney* of *London*, till they had other Commandement from him and his *Counsell:* Because *Verney* being indebted to the King, and others, practised to be indicted of *Felony;* wherein he might have his *Clergie*, and make his purgation, of intent to defraud [*137] his Creditors; 34. *Henry* 6. *Rotulo* 37. *in Banco Regis.*

According to this *Moderation*, King *Edward* the 4. and his *Counsell* heard the *Cause* of the *Master* and *poore Brethren* of the *Hospitall* of St. *Leonards* in *Yorke;* complaining, That Sir *Hugh Hastings*, *Iohn Wombell*, and others, withdrew from them a great part of their living, which consisted chiefly upon having of a Thrave(†) of Corne of each Plow-land, within the Counties of *Yorke*, *Westmerland*, *Cumberland*, and *Lancashire;* and for the which, they being very poore men, were not able to sue the redresse at the *Common Law*, *Rotulo Paten. de Anno* 8. *Edward* 3.[87] *part* 3. *memb.* 14. And yet had they of that *Hospitall* a speciall Act of *Parliament* made for them, to give them *Action* in that very Case, 2. *Henry* 6. *cap.* 2.

[*138] According to the same *Moderation*, the same King and his *Councell* made a Decree(‡) for *Richard* the *Abbot* of Saint *Edmonds-Bury*, against *Walter Thurstone*, *William Sigo*, and others, the inhabitants of *Bury*,[88] whom he there punished, for turbulent elections of their *Aldermen*,[89] *Constables*, and

(†) A Thrave hath 24. sheaves, as a Stack hath 12.

(‡) *See Holling. Cron. p.* 344. *sur Records de Burie* 1. *Ed.* 3.

---

86 the] *H WF;* his *F.*

87 Edward 3.] Ed. 4. *F H WF.*

88 Bury] *F;* the Towne of Bury *H WF.*

89 Aldermen] *F H;* Alderman *WF.*

other *Officers;* whereas they had no Corporation at all, nor any other *Head*, besides the *Abbot. Rot. Paten. Anno* 20. *Edward* 4. *Part* 2.

According to the same *Moderation*, King *Henry* 7. and his *Councell*, in the first yeere of his reigne, heard the *Cause* of *Sanctuarie* at *Culvam*, claimed for Treason by *Humfrey Stafford*, under colour of the *Priviledges* of the *Abbey* of *Abbington;* and gave order, that the *Iudges* should deliberate thereupon; that *Stafford*, with his learned *Councell*, should be heard before them, and [*139] that the *Abbot* should be called to shew his *Priviledges*.

In which yeere also, a *Privie Seale* was awarded to the *Maier* of *Bristow, Ad faciendam Iustitiam;* to *Ferdinando de Saint Iago*, a *Spaniard;* or otherwise, to appeare *coram Rege*.

And likewise, the[90] same yeere the Kings *Councell* decreed, that *Margery* and *Florence Becket* should sue no further in their *Cause* against *Alice Radley*, widdow, for Lands in *Wolwich*, and *Plumstead;* for so much as that matter had been heard first before the *Councell* of King *Edward* 4. After that, before the *President* of the *Requests*(†)[91] of that King *Henry* 7. and then lastly, before the *Councell* of the same King.

And to conclude, I have seene it registred, That the same King *Henry* the seventh, did personally sit in *Iudgement*, with his *Councell*, in the *Star-chamber*, twelve severall times [*140] within the compasse of that first and second yeere of his Reigne; where according to his[92] *moderation*, the *Plaintiffe* was commonly bound either alone, or with *Sureties*, to justifie the matter of[93] *Complaint;* or otherwise, to pay *Costs* and *Expences* of the *Defendant;* and in default of such proofe, was many times committed to prison for his wrongfull vexation.

(†) President of the Requests.

---

90 the] *F;* in the *H WF.*

91 President of the Requests, *in the margin*] *F; om. H WF.*

92 his] *F H;* this *WF.*

93 of] *F;* of his *H WF.*

The *Defendant* likewise, most commonly, gave *Bond* for the *Peace*, or for the *Good abearing*, as the case required, to prevent all danger of force, and disturbance of the *Common Law;* whereunto, for tryall, they both were oftentimes dismissed.

But amongst other things which it hath chanced me to see, that order which the *Councell* during the minoritie of *Henry 6.* did set downe to be observed amongst themselves, is no lesse memorable than serviceable [*141] for this purpose: The which, although it doe containe some Articles not altogether proper to this Argument; yet for as much as it hath many points well tempered for the maintenance of this *Moderation*, and the same so interlarded with the rest, that it should be violent to dissever them; I will set it downe wholly, as it came to my hands.

ORDER TAKEN FOR THE
COUNCELL, DURING THE
Minoritie of King
Henry the sixt.

1 *That the Lord of* Bedford, *of* Glocester, *nor other of the* Councell *shall behote any favour, but that each* Bill *and* Suit *shall be seene by all the* Councell, *and by them to have reasonable* Answer.

[*142] 2 *That in the plaine* Terme *the* Councell *shall one day in the Weeke intend to the reading and answering of* Bills; *which* Answer *shall be endorsed on the* Bill *by the* Clarke *of the same* Councell, *and on the* Friday *declare it*[94] *to the partie suing, unlesse the great and notable Causes of the* Realme *let it.*

3 *All* Bills *comprehending matters terminable at the* Common Law, *shall be remitted thither, unlesse the discretion*

---

[94] declare it] *F;* declared *H WF.*

of the Councell *feele too great might on the one partie, and unmight on the other, or cause reasonable to move them.*

4 *No* Councellor *take upon him to be partie in any matter, there to be sped, but if it touch himselfe; and then he not to be present, while it is in hearing.*

5[95] *Each* Councellor *shall have full freedome to speake what he thinketh, in the matters demanded there, and none* [*143] *other of the said* Councell *shall conceive indignation; therefore*[96] *alwayes due reverence kept to every estate and person.*

6 *For avoiding of anger,*[97] *and indignation of persons out of the* Councell, *by discoverie of things spoken, and treated there; no person whatsoever shall abide in the* Councell, *while matters of the* Councell *be treated, save onely the* Councellors *sworne.*

7 *No* matter *shall be* assented, *but at the least there* assent *thereunto foure* Councellors, *and an* Officer, *assembled in the* forme *of* Councell, *and at a place*[98] appointed; *and that shall not suffice, unlesse they make the more part of the number then present in* Councell.

8 *No* Bill *be sped, but in place ordained for* Councell, *and the* Councell *being there in forme of a* Councell, *and the* Bill *to be read there first before them all, whereunto every man* [*144] *shall singularly say his advice; and then it may bee subscribed by the* Lords *there, or in any other place, where the* Clarke *of the* Councell *shall bring it himselfe unto him.*[99]

9 *The correction or removing of any* Councellor, *or great* Officer *of the King, shall proceed of the advice and*

---

[95] *F fails to number this item, so that the next is 5, and so on, in F alone.*

[96] *H WF place the punctuation here rather than before* therefore.

[97] of anger] *F;* mauger *H WF.*

[98] at a place] *H WF;* at the time *F.*

[99] him] *F;* them *H WF.*

assent of the more part of all those that had been appointed of the Kings Councell.

10 *All matters touching the King, shall be preferred to*[1] *all other, both in* Parliament *and* Councell.

11 *To* Benefices *and* Offices *becomming void, and belonging to the Kings disposition, those shall be preferred that have served the King or his predecessors; so that there be found among them persons able thereto.*

12 *Out of the* Terme-time, *nothing shall be sped in this* Councell, *but such things for the good of the King, and the*[2] *Land, that aske necessarie speed,* [*145] *and may not godly*[3] *be abidden unto the* Terme-time.

13 *If the* Opinions *of my Lord of* Bedford, *or of* Glocester, *fall on the part of the lesse number, and yet doe move the greater number forthwith to condescend; then shall the matter dwell in deliberation, till the next day; at which every man shall say his reason, and then shall stand the* opinion *of the more part in number: and if the number be equall, then shall that partie on which the Lord of* Bedford *or* Glocester *is in, be holden for the more partie.*[4]

14 *Where the Kings* Prerogative, *or* Free-hold, *is in question, there the Kings* Iudges *shall be called, and their* names *and* advices *shall be entred of* Record.

15 *The* Clarke *of the* Councell *shall be sworne, That each day of sitting, hee shall cause the* Bills *of the poorest* Suitors *to be first read, and answered, so neere as he can aske, or enquire; and* [*146] *the Kings* Sergeant *to be sworne, to give* Counsell *without* Fee, *to such as shall be accepted for poore, upon paine to be discharged of their* Offices.

16 *No Lord of this* Councell *shall wittingly receive, cherish, hold in household, nor maintaine any* Piller, Robber,

---

1 to] *F;* before *H; om. WF.*
2 the] *F;* his *H WF.*
3 godly] *F;* goodly *H WF.*
4 for the more partie] for the most part *F;* the more partie *H WF.*

Oppressor, Man-slayer, Felon, Outlaw, Ravisher, unlawfull Hunter, open misdoer, *or other, openly named or famed for such, till his* innocencie *be declared: Nor shall take any other mans* Cause, *or* Quarrell, *into favour, by* word, deed, *or* message, *by giving* Liverie, *or otherwise, by any* colour, *or* occasion *of* feoffement, gift, *or* Deed *of Lands, or moveables; nor shall conceive indignation against any* Iudge, *or* Officer, *for doing his* Office *in forme of* Law; *and shall cause their servants, and all others in their Countries, to doe the like.*

17 *No Lord of this* Councell *shall by* colour, *or* occasion *of* feoffement, [*147] *or gift of Lands, or other goods, receive, or take by himselfe, or by any other, to his use, any thing that shall stand in debate, or demand; without it be first spoken of, and committed to the Kings* Councell, *and by the more part of them considered to be lawfull to doe.*

18 *None of the said* Councell *shall by himselfe, or by any other, take any* gift, *for favour, or furthering of any person, or matter; upon paine to restore the double to the partie, sixe times as much to the King, and to be forbidden to sit in the said* Councell, *till the King be otherwise advised.*

Thus having made it clearely to appeare, who is, and ought to bee *Iudge*[5] of these *Complaints;* let us now also discover what is, and hath beene the most usuall Place for the exhibition of them.

[*148] THE[6] THIRD PART, TOUCHING THE PLACE.[6]

It must be true, that the *King* and his *Councell* are not to bee tyed to any one place, seeing that the place it selfe neither addeth, nor derogateth to, or from their *authoritie;* and there be many causes of remove and change, from place to place: But yet, even as the *Palace* at *Westminster* hath evermore beene reputed the chiefe Royall Seat of the Realme, as being most fre-

---

[5] Iudge] *F;* the Iudge *H WF.*

[6] The . . . place] *F WF; om. H. F alone places this heading before the preceding sentence.*

quented with the personall presence of the Kings, and honoured with the Solemnity of *Coronations*[7] and assemblies of Estates in Parliament; so the *Councell-Chamber* of that *Palace* hath obtained that[8] dignitie, to beare a name above all others, and hath beene of long time called the *Star-Chamber*.

[*149] THE[9] STAR-CHAMBER IS THE USUALL PLACE.[9]

It[10] is said in the *close Roles de Anno* 41. *Edw.* 3. That the same King, upon the fourth day of *May*, in the fortieth yeere of his reigne, received the *Complaint* offered by *Elizabeth*, the widdow of *Nicholas Audley*, whereof I have spoken; and thereupon caused *Iames Audley* to appeare before his *Councell, (viz.)* his *Chancellor*, *Treasurer*, *Iustices*, and other *Sages* assembled, *En la Chambre des Estoyers*[11] *pres de la resceipt al Westm.* in the *Chamber* of the[12] *Stars* neere the *Receipt* at *Westminster:* And the *Roll*, of *Patents de Anno* 2. *Richard*, *part* 1. *membr.* 28. hath the expresse name of the *Starre-Chamber.*

Furthermore as it appeareth by *Record*, that the same purgation [*150] of *Robert Danvers*, which I have before mentioned, was made the 20. of *Iune*, *Anno* 11. *Hen.* 6. *in Camera Stellata coram Consilio Regis.*

So was that *fraud* aforesaid of *Iohn Foard*, detected and punished in the *Star-chamber*, within the Kings *Palace* at *Westminster;* as by the *Close Roll de Anno* 17. *Hen.* 6. it is recorded.

It is moreover noted, That upon the 28. day of *November*, 28. *Hen.* 6. the Kings *Councell* being assembled in the *Councell-House*, called the *Star-chamber* at *Westminster; William*

---

[7] Coronations] the Coronations *F;* their Coronations *H WF.*

[8] that] *F;* the *H WF.*

[9] The . . . place] *F; om. H;* The Starre Chambre *WF* (*placing it a few lines earlier*).

[10] It] For it *F H WF.*

[11] Estoyers] *F;* estoiels *H WF.*

[12] of the] *F;* of *H WF.*

Talbois, of *Southkind* in *Lincolnshire*, came accompanied with many riotous persons, arrayed in warlike sort, and attempted to have slaine the said *Ralph*, Lord *Cromwell*, of whom I told you before, being one of the Kings *Councell*, and then sitting in *Councell* there, in the Kings *Palace*.

[*151] I finde likewise, That upon the 21. day of *November*, 32. *Hen.* 6. *Richard*, the Duke of *Yorke*, being called before the Kings great *Councell* by *Privie Seale*, in the *Star-chamber* at *Westminster*, complained, That his learned *Councell* was withdrawne from him; and therefore prayed,[13] they might without impediment resort unto him againe: Whereunto the Lords assented, and commanded, that the same their *assent* should be entred amongst the *Acts* of[14] *Councell*.

It appeareth also, That upon the first day of *Easter-Terme*, 35. *Hen.* 6. at *Westminster*, in the *Star-chamber*,[15] before the *Councell* of the King, a *Writ* of *Proclamation*, awarded by them against *Iohn* the Duke of *Norfolke*, was adnulled; because the first *Writ* issued upon the *Statute* of *Riots*, made 31. *Hen.* 6. *cap.* 2. and contained in it selfe no mention [*152] of *Riots*, and other the *Contents* of that *Statute*.

After the time of King *Henry* the sixth, this place was frequented for the like service by King *Edward* the 4. who, in the eighth yeere of his Reigne, sate there personally in *Councell*, attended with the *Archbishop* of *Yorke*, the *Bishop* of *Durham*, *Bath*, and *Rochester*, and the Earle of *Warwicke*, &c. there[16] decreed that *Cause* of the *Master* and *Brethren* of Saint *Leonards Hospitall*, of which I have used some mention before.

And in the 20. yeere of the reign of the same King, was that other *Decree* published in the *Star-Chamber*, which I noted before to have been made for the *Abbot* of Saint *Edmonds*-

[13] prayed,] *F;* prayed that *H WF.*
[14] of] *F;* of the *H WF.*
[15] Star-chamber] *F;* Starred Chamber *H WF.*
[16] there] *F;* and there *H WF.*

Bury, against the inhabitants of the same Towne. Of which King also, the *Chiefe Iustice*, 1 *Henry* 7. 3. reporteth, That he sate and conferred with his *Nobility* in the *Star-Chamber*, [*153] about the Execution of sundry *Statute-Lawes;* for the better observation of which, hee there tooke the Corporall Oathes of them all.

But to omit that of *Rich.* 3. and sundry other *Records* of other times, concurring in the same testimonie, those twelve severall stately *Sessions*, honoured with the Royall presence of King *Henry* 7. and sometimes with almost forty of his *Councell*, in the 1. and 2. yeeres of his Reigne, whereof I spake, and sundry others performed by his *Chancellors* and *Councell* in the same place, doe assuredly[17] teach, that it was the ordinarie *Councell Chamber* of the King, whensoever he and his Court did lye, and sojourne at his *Palace*, in *Westminster*, frequented no lesse for deliberation on matters of estate, than for decreeing extraordinarie *Suits* and *Causes* of *Complaint.* [*154] And I thinke it no doubt, but that *Iudge Shard*, which 28. *Lib. Assis. Pl.* 52. openeth the severall significations of the words *Coram nobis*, in the Kings *Writs*, meanes[18] this place, when hee saith, that *Coram nobis*, without any more, requireth an appearance before the *King* and[19] his *Chamber*, even as *Coram nobis ubicunque, &c.* commandeth in the *Kings Bench, &c.*[20] and *Coram nobis in Cancellaria* willeth it before the Lord *Chancellour.*

The Name of Star-chamber.

But from whence this place first purchased the name of *Starchamber*, there may be divers conjectures; one, by derivation from the old *English* word *Steoran*, which signifieth to steare, or rule, as doth the *Pilot* in a *ship;* because the *King* and *Councell* doe sit here, as it were [*155] at the *Sterne*, and doe gov-

[17] assuredly] most assuredly *F H WF.*

[18] meanes] meaneth *F H WF.*

[19] and] *F;* in *H WF.*

[20] &c.] *F; om. H WF.*

erne the *Shippe* of the *Common-wealth:* Then, of the *Latine* word *Stellio*, which betokeneth that *starry* and *subtile Beast*, of whose name the fault of craftie Cozenage is borrowed by the *Civillians*, which they call *Crimen stellionatum*, because the *Sinne*[21] is punished in this Court by an extraordinary *paine*, even as it was in the *Law Civill.*

Lastly, because happily the Roofe thereof was at the first garnished with gilded *Stars*, as[22] the *Roome* it selfe is *starry*, or full of *Windows* and *Light;* in which respect, some of the *Latine Records* name it *Camera Stellata;* the *French*, *Le Chamber des Estoyels;* and the *English*, the *Starred Chamber;* as you may observe by that I have spoken before.

[*156] THE ANCIENT USAGE OF THE STARRE-CHAMBER.[23]

But leaving the choyce of these, as also all further conjecture therein, to other men; I will proceede to set forth the usage of proceeding in this place, before the making of the *Statute* 3. *Hen.* 7. *cap.* 1. the which, some men (but much deceived) doe take to have laid the first stone of this farre more ancient and stately Erection.

Upon *Complaint* exhibited,[24] the Plaintiffe either came freely,[24] or was sent for by *Corpus cum causa*, if hee were in prison: The Defendant was summoned, or called in, either by *Writing*, or *Messenger;* by *Writing*, as by the Kings owne *Letter;* or by his *Privy Seale*, directed under a peine to the partie [*157] selfe, or to the *Sheriffe*, to take *Sureties* for his appearance; or by *Letters missive*, from the *Councell;* and if hee made default, then upon *Affidavit* made, by an *Attachment* and *Proclamation* of *Rebellion*, if the case require it. By moni-

---

21 Sinne] *F;* same *H WF.*

22 as] *F WF;* and *H.*

23 *F H here add:* before the Stat. 3. Hen. 7. Cap. 1; *WF adds:* before .3. H. 7.

24 exhibited . . . freely,] *H WF;* exhi- *F* (*with* bited, *as catchword, so evidently an omission in F of the next page's first line in print*).

tion of a *Messenger*, as by a *Sergeant* at *Armes;* who, upon contempt of former *Processe*, or upon doubt of the flying of the partie, or for his being neere at hand, or in respect of the hainousnesse of the fact, was many times addressed to seize upon the Defendant, and to bring him into the Court.

The *Pleading* was by *Bill*, *Answer*, and *Replication*, as by the *Records* of these two Cases of S. *Edmonds-Bury* and S. *Leonards Hospital*, before mentioned, I doe plainely find.

The *Hearing* was aswell by examination upon *Oath* of the *Defendants* [*158] themselves, as of their witnesses; against whom the manner was to award compulsaries for their appearance, if the party would depose their testimony to be necessary for him, and if their ability of body would beare the travaile: if not, then were they, in pitty of their impotency, examined at home.

The *Determination*, was by *Decree*, which passed by the assent of the more part, delivering their *opinions* singularly; whereby either the *Cause* was decided in the *Court*, or dismissed to *tryall* at the *Common Law;* or otherwise, upon default of the *plaintiffe* (being proclaimed, or called thrice at the *Councell doore*) the *Defendant* was quite *dismissed*, with his *costs* and *expences*.

[*159] THE OFFICERS OF THE STAR-CHAMBER.

The *Officers*, or Ministers that I finde, were then the *Usher*, the *Serjeant* at *Armes*, the *Atturneyes*, and the *Clarke*. The *Usher*, for the keeping of the *roome*, the proclaiming of silence, the calling of names, and other base *services*, and the *Serjeant*, as well to beare the *Mace*, for the honor of the *Lord Chancellor*, as[25] to *arrest* and bring such as he was commanded.

Touching the *Atturneyes*, I wot not whether their *Service* might then be called a standing *office*, or no, because they were

---

[25] as] as for *F H WF*.

at large, some[26] two or three at once being received, to follow for one *Clyent;* in so much, as there were above thirtie severall *persons* imployed thereabouts, during onely the first and second yeares of *King Hen.* 7.

Clarke of the Star-Chamber.[27]

[*160] The *Office* of the *Clarke* of the *Councell,* was to *Take, Endorse, Enter, Keepe,* and *Certifie* the *Bills, Pleadings, Records, Rules,* and *Decrees* of the Court. And as it is not to bee doubted, but there hath beene from time to time, a *Clarke* of the *Councell,* considering that such a Court could not be without the service of such a *Minister,* (albeit happily his *authoritie,* in examining of *Witnesses,* taking of *Affidavits,* and admitting men by *Atturney,* was by little and little enlarged): So I doe not finde it expressed, who was the *Clarke* during the minority of *King Hen.* 6. or at any time before it; For the very first of whose name I have read, was *Thomas Kent,* a *Doctor* of the *Law,* to whom King *Henry* the sixt, by his *Letters Patents,* dated the fifteenth of *Iuly,* in the two and twentieth yeare of his raigne, gave both that Office for his life, calling [*161] him *Clericum Consilii nostri,* and the *Office* of the *Secundarie* of the *Privie Seale;* with *wages,* of a hundred pounds by yeare; and with *power,* for reasonable cause of absence, to make his sufficient *Deputie* therein. After him, whether immediately or no, I have not to affirme, because that I suspect that one *Langport* was betweene, in the first yeare of King *Henry* the seventh; *Iohn Bladswell,* a *Doctor* of the *Lawes* also, was made *Clarke* of the *Councell,* and exercised the same *Office:* The degrees of which two men, whereof the first was afterwards sworne[28] of the *Councell,* doe set forth the *dignitie* of the *place,* being (as I suppose) the best *Clarkeship* of this *Land,*

---

26 some] *F;* sometymes *H WF.*

27 Clarke of the Star-Chamber.] *om. F H WF.*

28 sworne] *F WF; om. H.*

unlesse you will call the Master of the *Rols* a *Clarke* againe; as some former *Statutes* are wont to name him.

And these bee the onely named men of that *place*, with whom I have [*162] yet met, before that *Statute* made in the third yeare of King *Henry* the seventh.

After whom, that I may shortly *summon* them all, there succeeded in the sixt yeare of King *Henry* the seventh, *Robert Riden;* in the first yeare of King *Henry* the eight, *Iohn Meutis, Secretarie* for the *French;* and in the fourth yeare of the same King, *Richard Eden:* during one time of whose sicknesse, *Thomas Eliot* held the Place: in the 22. yeare of which King also, the *Office* was upon a surrender, granted jointly to that *Richard Eden*, and *Thomas Eden*, which last man forthwith exercised the same alone. And[29] in the fifth yeare of King *Edward* the sixt, it was granted in reversion, after the death of that *Thomas Eden*, to *Thomas Marsh*, to whom it fell in possession, in[29] the ninth yeere of her Majestie[30] that now is: In like reversion, after [*163] whose death, it was likewise granted to[30] *William Mills*, mine[31] ancient favourer, a man trained up from his youth in the services of that Court; who tooke it in possession the fifteenth yeare of her Highnesse Reigne, and now holdeth: By whose good *labours* and *friendships* also, I was the better enabled to write some part of this present Discourse.[31]

THE[32] AUTHORITIE OF THE STAR-CHAMBER BY NEW STATUTES[32]

But having now[33] runne through the ancient usage of this[34]

---

[29] And . . . in] *F WF;* and held it till *H.*

[30] Majestie . . . granted to] *F WF;* Majesties Reigne; at which tyme Thomas Marshe succeeded, and after him followed *H.*

[31] mine . . . Discourse] *F WF;* who att this tyme filleth the Roome *H.*

[32] The . . . Statutes] *WF* (*WF reads* the new); *om. F H.*

[33] But having now] *F;* Havinge in this manner *H;* But now, having thus *WF.*

[34] this] *F WF;* this most stately *H.*

Court, there remaineth a consideration of that *Statute* made in the third yeere of King *Henry* the seventh; by which the persons therein named, are authorised[35] by their discretions,[36] to examine certain offences,[37] & the same to punish, according[38] to the effect of the [*164] *Statute-Lawes*,[39] the very words whereof be these.[39]

> The King our Soveraigne Lord remembreth, how by unlawfull *Maintenances*, giving of *Liveries*, *Signes*, and *Tokens*, and by *Retainders*, by *Indentures*, *Promises*, and other *Writings*, or otherwise, *Embraceries* of his *Subjects*, untrue demeaning of *Sheriffes*, in making *Pannels*, and other untrue *Returnes*, by taking of *Money* by *Iuries*, by great *Riots*, and unlawfull *Assemblies*, the policie and good rule of the *Realme* is almost subdued; and for not punishing those inconveniences, and by occasion of the premisses, nothing or little may be found by inquirie, whereby the *Law* of the *Land* in execution may take little effect, to the encrease of *Murthers*, *Robberies*, *Perjuries*, and unsuretie of all men [*165] living, and losses of their lands and goods, to the great displeasure of *Almightie God:* Therefore it is ordained, for reformation of the premisses, by authoritie of the said *Parliament*, That the *Chancellor*, and *Treasurer* of *England* for the time being, and *Keeper* of the Kings *Privie Seale*, or two of them (calling to them a *Bishop*, and a *Temporall* Lord, of the Kings most honourable *Privie*[40] *Councell*, and the chiefe *Iustices* of the *Kings Bench* and *Common Pleas*

---

[35] named, are authorised] *F WF;* specially named have Authority *H.*

[36] discretions] *F WF;* wisedomes and discrecions *H.*

[37] certain offences] *F WF;* sundry sorts of misdemeanors *H.*

[38] according] *F WF;* not arbitrably but accordinge *H.*

[39] Statute-Lawes . . . be these] *F WF* (*WF adds* viz.); Statutes thereof made, the lettre of which Statute standeth thus *H.*

[40] Privie] *F; om. H WF.*

> for the time being, or other two *Iustices*, in their absence) upon *Bill*, or *Information*, put to the said *Chancellor* for the King, or any other, against any person, for any misbehaviour aforesaid,[41] have *authoritie* to call before them, by *Writ* or *Privie Seale*, the said misdoers, and them, and others, by their [*166] discretions, by whom the truth may be knowne, to examine: and such as they finde therein defective, to punish them after their demerits, after the forme & effect of the *Statutes* thereof made, in like manner and forme as they should or ought to be punished, if they were thereof convict after the due order of the *Law*, *Anno. 3. Hen. 7. cap. 1.*

This *Statute*, as some have thought, was made for the restraint of that absolute *authoritie*, which before-time was exercised by the Kings *Councell:* So, as after the making hereof, they were to take knowledge of these few *Causes* onely, and of none others.

But I doe rather expound it by way of enlargement of their *Iuridicall authoritie:* for insomuch as there are not in it any words prohibitorie touching the former manner of proceeding; [*167] and the scope of this *Law*, is to have those *offenders* convicted by other meanes than by order of *Law*,[42] as they were before; I gather thereby, that the *Statute* giveth an *additament* of this sort: (*viz.*) That whereas before-time the King and the Lords of his *Councell* did not admit any *Complaint*, but such onely as carried within it a reasonable surmise of maintenance of their *Iurisdiction;* for the proofe whereof, also the Plaintife ought by the *Statute* 15. *Hen.* 6. *cap.* 4. to give *Sureties*, as I have before shewed. Now by this new *Statute*, over and besides that ancient *authoritie*, onely these three of the *Councell*, (*viz.*) the *Chancellor*, *Treasurer*, and

---

[41] aforesaid] *F;* afore rehearsed *H WF.*

[42] Law] *F;* the Lawe *H WF.*

Keeper of the *Privie Seale* (using the assistance of some *others* thereunto appointed) were enabled to *heare* & *determine* ordinarily of these 8. *offences*, and that without any manner of such suggestion, or [*168] surmise at all: And that both King *Henry* the seventh, and King *Henry* the eight, did many yeeres after the making of this *Statute*, sometime in person, and very often by their *Councell*, practise that by former *Iurisdictions*[43] in the *Star-Chamber*, without any help of this new *Law* & *Statute*, it doth most certainly appeare by the Bookes[44] of *Entries* kept there; which is a true *Ephemeris* or[45] *Iournall* of the *Acts* of the[46] *Court*.

But for as much as they of the *Parliament* holden in the 21. yeare of[47] King *Henry* the eight, *cap.* 20.[48] espyed some defects in this *Statute* of *Henry* the seventh, they did supply the same after this manner following; *viz.*

> The *Chancellor*, *Treasurer* of *England*, and the *President* of the K. most honorable *Privie Councell*, attending upon his most honorable *Person*, for the time being, [*169] & the *Keeper* of the K. *Privie Seale*, or two of them, calling unto them one *Bishop*, and one *temporall* Lord of the K. most honorable *Councell*, and the two chief *Iustices* of the *Kings Bench*, & the *Common Pleas*, for the time being or other two of the K. *Iustices* in their absence, upon any *Bill* of *Information* hereafter to be put in: The *Chancellor* of *England*, *Treasurer*, *President* of the K. said most honorable *Councell*, or *Keeper* of the K. *Privie Seale* for the time being, for any misbehavior[49] before rehearsed, from henceforth have full *power* and *authoritie* to cal before them by *Writ* of *Privie Seale*, such

---

[43] that by former Iurisdictions] *F;* that former Iurisdiction *H WF.*

[44] Bookes] *F;* booke *H WF.*

[45] Ephemeris or] *WF; om. F;* or *H.*

[46] the] *F;* that *H WF.*

[47] of] *F;* of the Reigne of *H WF.*

[48] cap. 20.] *om. F H WF.*

[49] misbehavior] *F;* misbehavinge *H WF.*

misdoers, and them, and other, by their discretion, by whom the *truth* may be knowne, to examine: And such as they shall find defective, to punish them after their demerits, after the [*170] forme and effect of the said former *Statute*, and of all other *Statutes* thereof before made, & not repealed, & expired, in like manner and forme, as they should or ought to bee punished, if they were thereof convicted after the due order of the *Kings Lawes*.

By which latter Statute these things following are brought to passe, *viz.* first, that the *President* of the Kings *Councell* is hereby added to that *triumvirate*, and is made one of the *Iudges* of[50] them.

Secondly, a doubt is here taken away, that might be moved upon the words of the first *Statute*, namely, whether the *Bishop*, the temporall Lord of the Kings *Councell*, and the *Iustices*[51] named in that *Statute*, were *Iudges* equall in his[52] *Authoritie*, with the other three great *Officers;* or else whether they were but onely assistant unto them with their advice: [*171] For here, in this latter *Law* the full *authoritie* is given onely to those three, and the *President;* so as the residue are to be called onely for their advice: But yet so, that the proceeding is erroneous, if either the other foure doe not call them, or doe not heare their advice when they be called.

Lastly, the Bill, or information, ought by this latter *Statute* to bee put in generally, that is, to the King, as it was wont to be: Whereas, by the strict words of the former Act, the same was to have been exhibited to the Lord *Chancellour:* And thus by the benefit of these two *Statutes*, the judiciall handling of these eight offences which before did proceed, as I partly touched, either by way of Indictment, or Action, may now be performed without any *Enquest* or *Verdict*, even by the onely

---

[50] of] *F;* with *H WF.*
[51] and the Iustices] *H WF; om. F.*
[52] his] *F;* this *H WF.*

examination either of [*172] competent witnesses of[53] the parties themselves, or of both; a course which was never before permitted by the *Common Law* of the *Realme*, wherein no *Tryall* was allowed; but that only *per legale Iudicium parium*, as the *Great Charter* it selfe plainly doth acknowledge.

And this was now at the last devised, because as the *Statutes* themselves doe report, that ancient and ordinary proceeding at the *Common Law*, against these *Maintainers*, *Reteyners*, *Ryoters*, and the rest of that[54] *rabble* was hindered by the greatnesse of the *Offenders*, which were belike so *brested*, *sided*, and *backed* with a many[55] *friends*, *tenants*, and *followers* in their owne Countries, that none *Indictment* or *tryall* could make the way to touch them: Which thing threatned the utter subversion of the good *policie* of the *Realme*, if this soveraigne and higher hand [*173] had not been timely extended for help and remedie.

Howbeit[56] by the expresse words of these new Lawes, these offences named in them, are in none other degree to be punished in this *Court* now, than they were before upon conviction by judgement, and the tryall of twelve.

The double[57] Authoritie of the *Star-Chamber*.[57]

And therefore the change that is offered, resteth cheifly in the circumstances of place, Processe, Iudges,[58] and meane of tryall, the very substance it selfe (that is to say) the discretion of the fault it selfe, and the distribution of the paine due thereunto, remaining the very same that they were before; from the which appointed paines, if these Lords shall at any time think good to varie and depart, then it must be understood to be done by that former *authority* which they had, and have

53 of] *F;*, or of *H WF.*
54 that] *H WF;* the common *F.*
55 a many] *F;* a manie of *H WF.*
56 *H alone here has as section heading:* What change the Statute 3. Henry 7. hath wrought.
57 The double . . . Star-Chamber] *WF; om. F H.*
58 Iudges] *H WF; om. F.*

as the Councell of the King, [*174] and not by vertue of these *Statutes*, which doe leave unto them no liberty at all in this behalfe, for wee[59] may not so conjoyne, or rather confound these Authorities, as either of them shall be extinct, and[60] drowned in the other, but wee must preserve them both separably,[61] and distinct, not onely in understanding, but in the[62] execution and practice also; even as when the *Iustices* that ride the Circuits, doe bring with them into the Countrie one *Commission* of *Oyer* and *Terminer*, and another of *Gaole Deliverie*, and a third of the *peace*, and doe sit upon the tryall of *Felonies*, they may lawfully extend their authoritie by the one, where the other will not reach, and serve the businesse; which thing, they could not do if by such a Conjunction the greater *Commission* should be said, to devoure and swallow the lesse.

[*175] A Confutation of some Objections against the Star-chamber.

And this one hold is of sufficient strength to withstand the Assaults of all those objections which some are wont to make against certaine the proceedings in this Court.

For whereas they doe thinke that none other Complaints can be sentenced here, but these onely, which are in[63] these *Statutes*, or some other[64] specially appointed to be thus determined, they bee deceived, for that they doe not cast their eyes upon that former power, which these Lords and others doe bring hither with them, as the *Councell* of the *Queen*, the which is not to be restrained to these so narrow bounds. And no lesse doe some others erre in judgement, which doe maintaine, that without the presence of some [*176] two of these

---

59 *The heading above is located actually in the margin here, both in T and WF.*

60 and] *F;* or *H WF.*

61 separably] *F;* separable *H WF.*

62 in the] in *F H WF.*

63 in] *F;* by *H WF.*

64, or some other] *F;* (or some other) *H WF.*

foure Lords mentioned in the last *Statute*, no Decree made in this Court is warranted by the *Law*, for they are convicted by the same[65] former reason; considering that the *Councell*[66] of the *Queene* (sitting there in forme of a *Councell*) are not deprived of that ancient *authoritie*, by the absence of any two or three of them.

More[67] probably I confesse, doe those men reason, who (pressing this Court with the words of these *Statutes*, and with the generall usage of all other Courts of *Iustice*) doe thinke that a *Bill*, or *Information* in writing is so necessary, for setting the *Complaint* on foot there, as that without it, the proceeding verbally, (or *Ore tenus* as wee call it) is not in any case to bee allowed.

It is true, that the hearing and determining causes upon Bills and [*177] answers[68] in *writing*, is generally a very sure manner of proceeding, as well for the cutting off[69] of all tergiversation, and cavelling between the *parties*, as for the *Warrant* and *defence* of the *Iudges* themselves. But yet it seemeth to mee that in speciall *Cases* this Court both hath sufficient authoritie, and may of[70] good discretion take knowledge of the cause, and decree punishment for it, without any such information of the *matter* set down in *writing*; for as all the *travell* and *labours*[71] of whatsoever *Iudges* ought to bee directed to this only end, and marke, that (the *truth* of the *Controversie* being found out)[72] *Iustice* may bee delivered, and as in a *Criminall Complaint* (which is the proper subject of this Court) the *truth* can no way better appeare, than by *Confession* of the *Offender* himselfe. So if either the necessitie [*178] of the *Cause* doe

[65] the same] *H WF;* some *F.*

[66] Councell] *F H;* Counseilors *WF.*

[67] *H alone here has the heading:* Informacion Ore tenus.

[68] causes upon Bills and answers] *F;* of Causes uppon Bill and Answer *H WF.*

[69] off] *F; om. H WF.*

[70] of] by *F H WF.*

[71] travell and labours] travells, and Labours *F;* travaile and labor *H WF.*

[72] out] *F; om. H WF.*

require, that the guilty party be speedily convented[73] or charged, or if he be deprehended *flagranti crimine*, in committing the *fault*, or if the *offence* doe onely, or chiefly concerne her *Majestie*, or if the circumstances thereof, be such as may not seemely abide the blazing of a *Bill*, and then the *Offender* shall, upon *Examination*, freely, and without torture, confesse the *body* and *substance* of the *crime* that is verbally laid to his charge, surely neither he, nor any for him, can justly complaine of *Injustice*, in that he is *sentenced* without *Bill*, and *answer* in *writing:* Wherefore[74] when *Iustice* is once satisfied, I see none other use, but onely for a memoriall, in which behalfe the *proceeding* it selfe being entred in the Records of the Court, shall be an *act* of equall credit, with that, that begun[75] by *Bill* in *writing:* and it is [*179] plaine, that *Bill* and *Answer* in *writing* be not of the substance, but only of the solemnitie, and ceremonie of *judiciall proceedings*, the which also may best be spared in *Criminall Causes*, in which otherwise the delivery of *Iustice* may sometimes be hindred by over-much formality.

For which cause as I think, King *Edward* 1. in that place of *Britton*, which I have cited, sticketh not to affirme, that it belongeth to his Kingly Office, to give due *Iudgement* wheresoere the very *truth* doth appeare, *sans auter proces*, without any other *Formality*, *Ceremony*, *Solemnity*, or *Proces* at all. And therefore, if after a *Bill* exhibited here, and the matter of *Complaint* proved by *Examination* of the party, and by deposition of *Witnesses*, it should fortune, the *Bill*, or other parts of the *Pleading* to bee imbezelled or lost; I would not doubt, but that this [*180] Court (which must not alwayes be tyed to the strict order of *Pleading*, that is necessary to be observed in some other Courts) might either cause a new *Bill* to be

---

[73] convented] *H WF;* committed *F.*

[74] Wherefore] whereof *F H WF.*

[75] that, that begun] those that begun *F;* those that beganne *H WF.*

framed upon the *matter* already proved, and brought to light, or else command the *Queenes Atturney* to enforme it *Ore tenus* verbally, without offer of any *Bill* at all. According to which summary manner of *Iudgement*, the *Kings Councell*, who have the exercise of the same, his owne *Authority* have many times proceeded in this Court: Whereof the Bookes of Entries there, hath plentifull Testimonies; which I for avoiding the odious *rehearsall* of mens names, not yet forgotten, doe willingly forbeare to produce.

Thus have I made it appeare[76] both what hath been the right usage of this Court, by the originall *power* thereof, and what accesse of *Authoritie* [*181] it hath received by these new *Lawes* and *Statutes;* the which were, as you see, ordained to apply a most honourable, high, awfull, and ordinarie remedie for these enormities and[77] excesses, which were at that time growne so exorbitant and high, that they might not sufficiently be revenged by the inferiour *Iudges*, and usuall stroake of the *Common Law*. In which case right necessary it was, that the *King* himselfe, and[78] such as were neerest in the staire of *Authoritie* underneath him, should shew themselves; by the *Majestie* and awe of whose *Personall State* and *Presence*, both these *Offenders* might bee abashed, and beaten down, and these *offences* might be made exemplary, and forewarning to other men.

[*182] The[79] severall Offences determinable by the Statutes.

And now so much being said touching these things, let us descend to the particular enumeration and handling of these *offences*, that are by the *Statute-Lawes* to be heard and de-

---

[76] it appeare] *F;* to appeare *H WF.*

[77] enormities and] *F WF; om. H.*

[78] and] *F;* or *H WF.*

[79] *Both F and H lack what our text now presents in its next forty-one pages.*

termined before the Lords here. And for as much as these two *Statutes* doe affoord us eight at one,[80] let them be ranged in the first place as they stand, *viz.*

Unlawfull Maintenance.
Giving of Liveries, Signes, or Tokens.
Reteiners by writing, or otherwise.
Embraceries of the Kings subjects.
Untrue demeanings of Sheriffes, in making Pannels, or other untrue Returnes.
Taking of Money by Iuries.
Great Riots, and unlawful[81] *Assemblies.*

[*183] All which also, are bent (as I said) either by fraud or force, to the hinderance of the execution of *Law*, and to the encrease (as one of these *Statutes* saith) of *Murthers, Robberies, Perjuries*, unsuretie of mens *lives*, and losse of their *goods* and *lands*. For the better manifestation of these matters, therefore I will lift them up by one and one in order as they lye; and will first shew the nature of each *fault;* then, the *evils* that doe ensue thereof: and lastly, the *punishment* that by *Law* is layd upon it.

Maintenance.

Maintenance seemeth to be derived of the *Latine* words, *Manu tenere;* because hee that maintaineth, taketh by the hand (as it were) and holdeth the *Cause* of another man as fast, as if it were his owne [*184] proper: and therefore *Maintenance* is a kind of *conspiracie* made by two or more *persons* against some *other;* because the very *partie* to the *Cause*, and that others[82] which steppeth into the furtherance of it, doe combine themselves together, and doe make a *Complot* against the

---

80 one] once *WF*.
81 and unlawful] Unlawful *WF* (*which starts a new line with it and, having numbered the foregoing, marks this as* 8.).
82 others] other *WF*.

adverse partie to the same. And this may be as well for matter hanging in *Suit*, or *Plea*, as for some other *Cause* not being brought in[83] *Plea*, or *Action*, howbeit, *Maintenance* is commonly understood of *Causes* in *Suit:* as when one that hath none *interest* to a matter in question, will either give *money* to *Councell*, or will take some *interest* of purpose, to make the *Cause* seeme to be his owne, or will shew himselfe (and give his *speech* or *countenance*) for the *one side*, at the time that the matter shall be *heard*, or *tryed;* or will *terrifie* or *discountenance* the *contrarie side;* or generally, will doe any thing [*185] for the *one partie*, to the hinderance of the free course of *Iustice* against the *other*.

Champartie.

Of this *Maintenance*, there is one sort that beareth a speciall name, and is called *Champartie;* because the partie to a *Suit* giveth to some other man (for *maintenance* sake) *Campi partem*, that is, some *part* of the thing in demand, or otherwise, some *profit* going out of the same. And *Champartors* (saith the *Statute* 3. *Ed.* 1.) be they that *move Pleas* and *Suits*, or cause them to be *moved* by their owne (or other mens procurement)[84] and *sue* them at their owne proper *Costs*, to have part of the *land* in variance, or part of the *gaines* that may come by the *Suit*.

The *persons* that fall into the *fault* of *Maintenance*, or *Champartie*, be eyther *publike* (as *Officers*) or else *private* men: And the *evils* that doe ensue thereof, be great in them both; [*186] but so much the greater in *publike* persons, as they have (which *private* men doe want) the helpe of their *Offices*, and aide of their *Authoritie*, to worke their harmes withall. For if it be permitted, that every one (and especially

---

[83] in] into *WF*.

[84] mens procurement)] mens) procurement *WF*.

such as have the higher *Places*) may step into the *Quarrell* of another, and *maintaine* it as his owne, both by his *Purse*, and other *Power;* then shall the *Cause* of the poore and honest be overthrowne, and trampled under foot, and then shall the *wicked* be imboldened to offer *injurie;* and the way to *redresse*, shall be shut up and fast barred. The *Lawes* of the *Realme* have therefore (according to the diversitie of the *offence* herein) ordained sundry and diverse *punishments:* And first, for *Maintenance*, thus:

None of the Kings *Councellors*, servants of his *Household*, [*187] *Officers* of his *Courts*, or great men of the *Realme*, shall take upon them to *maintaine* any *Quarrels* or *Parts* in the Countrey, to the disturbance of the *Common Law:* Upon paine, that every *Officers* Bodies,[85] Goods, & Lands shall be at the Kings pleasure, *1. Ed. 3. cap. 14. 4. Ed. 3. cap. 11. 20. Ed. 3. cap. 4. & 1. R. 2. cap. 4.*

No man shall by any meanes buy or sell, or take, promise, or covenant to have any pretended *Right* or *Title* to any *Lands*, *Tenements*, or *Hereditaments*, unlesse he that so selleth, promiseth or covenanteth, or his *Ancestors*, or they by whom hee claymeth, have beene in *possession* thereof, or of the *Reversion* or remainder thereof, or have taken the *Rents* or *profits* thereof by the space of one whole yeare next before such sale, covenant, or promise: upon [*188] paine, that such seller or promiser shall lose the whole value of the thing bought, or promised; and that such buyer or taker of promise (knowing hereof) shall likewise lose the whole value thereof.

No man shall by any sinister labour or meanes *maintaine* any *matter* or *cause*, to the disturbance or hinder-

---

[85] every Officers Bodies] their offices, bodies *WF.*

ance of *Iustice;* upon paine to lose *10. li.* for every offence, *32. H. 8. cap. 9.*

No *Sheriffe* or *Steward* of any *Court* shall suffer any *Barettor*, or *maintainer* of *Quarrels*, in their *Countrie*[86] *Courts*, or other *Courts;* upon paine, that the King shall grievously punish both the *Sheriffe* and him that so doth, *3. E. 1. cap. 32.*

No person (after *forcible entrie* by him made into any Lands, or after the holding the same with [*189] *force*) shal make any *feoffement* or *discontinuance* thereof (for *maintenance* sake) to any *Lord*, or other *person*, to defraud the *Possessor* of his *Recoverie:* And if it may be proved, then that *feoffement* or *discontinuance* shalbe *void*, *8 H. 6. c. 9.*

No person shal so *maintaine* any *Riot*, *Rout*, or *unlawfull Assembly*, that the same thereby may[87] be found by the *Iurie* (charged to inquire thereof) upon the paine of *imprisonment*, and to forfeit *20. li. 19. H. 7. cap. 13.*

Touching *Champartie*, it is ordained, that such as take *Pleas* to *Champartie* by any *craft* or *means*, shall (if they be any of the Kings *Councellors*, *Household servants*, *Iustices* of his *Courts*, or *ministers* there) have *3.* yeres *imprisonment*, and make *fine* at the K. pleasure, *21. E. 1.* & if they be other *persons* than such, then they shall forfeit so [*190] much of their owne Lands and Goods, as the thing (that they have so bought) shall be worth, *28. Ed. 1.*

Giving of Liveries.

Giving of *Liveries*, *Badges*, or other *signes* or *tokens*, is the next *fault* in order to *Maintenance*, and partaketh of the same

---

[86] Countrie] countie *WF.*

[87] may] may not *WF.*

nature, being also a sort of *Conspiracie* to *maintaine* some partie, and make it great withall; for on the one side, when *Noble* (or mighty men) and *Gentlemen* doe perceive that the tryall of *Causes* in the Countrie proceedeth ordinarily by the mouths of *Franklins* and *Yeomen* (*Free-holders*) and doe find themselves unable (without such) to cover their *wrongs* and *oppressions* with the Cloake of *Law:* Then doe they many times reteine such men into their *avowment*, *service*, [*191] and *protection;* offering unto them the countenance of their own *Nobility*, *Authoritie*, *Wealth*, and *Friends*, that they also may receive reciproque favour and good helpe by their sollicitation and meanes amongst the *Free-holders* of the Country that be their *Neighbours*, *Friends*, and *Kinsfolke.*

And on the other side these *Good fellowes*, seeing that the *Cloake* and *Cloth* of a *Noble man*, or other great *personage*, is a good defensative against such stormes of *Law* (or other businesses) as doe arise in the Country, and that *Might* doth many times (as the Proverbe is) overcome *Right*. They[88] also willingly and by great Suit emband themselves amongst their other servants; and many of them when they finde themselves so invested, wax afterwards as bold to offer wrong to their *Neighbours*, as they were glad [*192] at first to be shielded from it: Besides this, there was wont to be another kind of league and aliance, not of Master and Servant, but of equalls amongst themselves, whereof no lesse harme ensued than of the former: For the vulgar and base people, espying that the *Church-men* were rich and strong by their immunities, the *Nobility*, *Gentrie*, and best *Yeomandrie* of the Countrie were fast linked in bands together, and that in Cities and Corporate Townes also, there was an usuall combining of many into one body: So as[89] all other sorts of men (besides themselves) were strongly united, and they onely loose, and left to themselves:

---

[88] Right. They] right, they *WF*. [89] So as] So that *WF*.

They also fell therefore to shoaling and banding into *Companies*, and (each man at their owne charge) suited themselves in like *Coats*, *Hoods*, *Hats*, *Laces*, and other common *markes*, whereby [*193] they might be knowne each to other of them.

Now, albeit these *Conventions* may (at the first shew) deceive many, with a *Vizard* of *Amitie*, *Love*, and *Brotherhood;* yet the *wisdome* of the *Law* (that is able to unmaske such *fraud*) hath discovered many dangerous *evils*, that lye and lurke underneath them.

For, besides that the common course of *Iustice* betweene man and man, was greatly interrupted by these *Confederacies;* so as hardly any man that was not partie to such a *Conjuration*, could either aske his *Right* against any of them, or repell the injurie that they should offer unto him; the *Cause* of every one of them, being used as the *common Cause* and *Quarrell* of them all: It was found *perillous* (by many *proofes*) even to the *Estate* and *Kingdome* it selfe, that either *Noblemen* or *Gentlemen* [*194] should draw so long *Tailes* after them, or that the meaner sort of the people should be suffered to make so strong *Bodies* and *Bands* within themselves; both which, are the *Seed* and *Weed* of *Mutinie*, *Tumult*, and *Rebellion*. And therefore, the *Lawes* have armed their *power* against them; providing at the first,

> That no *Yeoman*, or other *person*, (under the degree of an *Esquire*) shal take any *Liverie* of any *Lord*, except he be his *Household servant*, or continual *Officer;* upon paine of *Fine* and *Imprisonment*, *16. R. 2. cap. 4. & 20. R. 2. cap. 2.*

Then afterwards it was ordained, upon the like paine,

> That no *Lord*, *Spiritual* or *Temporall*, should give *Liverie* to any *Knight* or *Esquire*, other than to his *Household*

servants, *Officers*, or *Councell* learned in the *Law*, *1. H. 4. cap.* 7.

Which *Law* stepped so far into this matter, [*195] that it forbad *Knights* and *Esquires* to weare the *Kings* owne *Liverie*, during the time that they had their aboade in their Countries. And King *Henry* the fourth seeing this *evill* to encrease, did also encrease the *paine*, and layd 5. *li.* upon the *giver* of every *Liverie*, (if he were a *Knight*, or under that estate) and 40. shillings upon the *taker*, 7. *Hen.* 4. *cap.* 14. At the length, the *penaltie* of 5. *li.* for every moneth, was inflicted upon the *giver*, and the like upon the *taker* of any *Liverie*, except he were his *Household-man*, *Officer*, or *Counsellor* at the *Law*, 8. *Ed.* 4. *cap.* 2. And because it was at the length perceived, that the *Officers* of the *Kings* owne *Castles*, *Mannors*, *Lands*, *Forrests*, *Chases*, and *Parkes*, were *retained* unlawfully by other men, and did also *retaine* into their owne *services* unlawfully the *Kings Fermors* and *Tenants;* those *offences* [*196] were also drawne into *Iudgement*, and *punished*, by the *losse* of those their *Offices* and *Leases*, 3. *H.* 7. *cap.* 12.

Thus farre of *Liveries*, *Signes*, or *Badges*, given by the *Superiour* to his *inferiour*.

As touching that other *confederacie* by[90] the *common people*, the same was also *prohibited*, under the *paine* of 40. s. laid upon every one that should *congregate* themselves by the use of any *common Liverie;* those *Fraternities* and *Mysteries* of *Cities* and *Boroughes* (that were ordained to a *good intent*) onely excepted, 7. *H.* 4. *cap.* 14.

And now it might seeme, that sufficient *Law* had bin provided against all kind of *Retainments:* but yet that was found true, which one said; *He that will devise* Law *against offences, hath the head of* Hydra *to fight withall;* seeing that one *evill* is no sooner cut off, but another starteth up, and taketh the

---

[90] by] of *WF*.

place. And even so fell it [*197] out in this matter of *Retainments:* For when the *Law* had laid sharpe *correction* upon the giving of *Liveries, Signes, Badges,* or other notorious *tokens* of *unlawfull complots;* then was it devised, that *men* should secretly *bind* themselves together (for *maintenance* of *Quarrels*) by *Oathes, Promises,* or *Writings;* whereof there grew a great deale more hurt, than of all the other *Retainers* besides: for that, in those other *Retainments,* men served at *libertie,* and might change when they would; but by this meanes they were so fast tyed, that without breach of *Oath,* or *Promise,* (things whereof all men use to make some *conscience*) they could not be set *free,* and *delivered:* And therefore, both such *Retainers,* and he that is *retained,* are to lose 100. s. for every *moneth* that such their *retainment* shall continue, 8. *Edw.* 4. *cap.* 2.

[*198] These be the *paines* that *Law* hath provided, and those be the *evils* that former times have espyed, concerning this matter of *Retainment.*

But yet there is, in time, a further *Mischiefe* begotten; the which if those *Lawes* had fore-seene, they would have *whetted* a sharper *edge* against it: For seeing that in former *Ages,* the *payment* of *Subsidies,* the *service* at *Musters,* and some other common *charges* of this our *time,* were not usuall; the *harme* of *Retainments* was not then so throughly seene and discovered, as now it is.

There is nothing more usuall at this day, than to *retaine* the wealthiest *Yeomanrie;* and either by forbearing them *wholly,* or charging them *lightly,* to make recompence of their *service,* by robbing the *Queenes Coffers,* or by defrauding *Her* and the *Realm* of that *help* which they might bring, if they were equally *burdened,* [*199] as their neighbours be, and not favoured by men that manage those *services,* in respect that they belong unto them. Which thing considered, it is to bee wished, that eyther sharper *Law* were provided, or (at the least) the[91] former *Law* more severely executed, against unlawfull *Retainments*. But now to the rest.

EMBRACERIE.

That *Embracerie* of the Kings *subjects*, which is mentioned in those *Statutes*, may be of two sorts: For either it may be taken for the drawing of *men* into *Bands* and *Companies*, for *maintenance* sake; and then it is but a *member* of the former *maintenance:* or else it may signifie, the *seducing* of *Iurors* to pervert *Iustice;* the which is more properly called, and most commonly known, by the name of *Embracerie*, and yet [*200] is a sort of *Maintenance*, and *Conspiracie* also: For in this respect, the *Statute* (28. *Ed.* 1.) called this sort of men, *false Informers*, and *Embraceours* of *Assises*, and *Iuries:* And the *Statute* (38. *Ed.* 3. *cap.* 13.) defineth them to be *Embraceours*, which doe sollicite and procure *Enquests* in the *Countrie*, to make *gaine* and *profit* thereby.

It tooke the name, and may well be derived, either of the *French* word *Embracer*, which is to *kindle* or set on *fire;* or else of the word *Embrasher*, of the same *Language*, which our *Tongue* hath *adopted*, and useth in the same *sence;* that is, where one man taketh another in his *armes*, and (as we usually speake) *embraceth* him: For by a *Metaphor*, of the first *meaning*, he that *laboureth* a *Iurie* for the *one side*, (or *partie*) may well be tearmed an *Embracer*, because he cannot doe it without *kindling* (or *incensing*) their [*201] *mindes* against the other *partie:* And by a *Metaphor*, of the second *meaning*, he may be said to be an *Embraceour* of a *Iurie*, that maketh *much* of them, and *embraceth* them in the *armes* of *faire speech*, *gifts*, or *promises;* to the end, to *allure* and *winne* them to the *one side*, against the *other*. So that, if a man will take upon him to *labour* and *plie* a *Iurie* for the *one side*, before they come to the *Barre;* or for[92] to *affray* them, when they be at the *Barre;*

---

[91] the] *om. WF.*

[92] for] seeke *WF.*

or by any meanes *endeavour* to *corrupt* them, for the *helpe* of the *one partie* against the *other;* hee is a speciall *Maintainer* under the name of *Embracerie.*

What *Evils* doe follow of this *fault*, may be seene by this, That it is a sort of *Maintenance;* and therefore sendeth abroad the like *effects*, in generalitie, that our *Maintenance*[93] have: But especially, it is *occupied* in [*202] corrupting of *Iurors*, which are (in effect) the very *Iudges* of our *Law*, seeing that the *Iudges* can give no other *sentence*, than according to the *Verdict* which the *Iurie* presenteth unto them.

Now what harmes may ensue by *poisoning* the *opinion* of *Iurers* in this *Realme* (wherein the chiefe proceeding in *Law* is by the meanes of them) every man may see, and (to say the truth) no lesse *mischiefe* doth accompanie it, than the secret undermining, ruine, and overthrow of all *Law, Right,* and *Iustice.*

Worthily therefore hath the *Law* (38. *Edw.* 3. *cap.* 12.) ordained,

> That if any person shall (for his owne gaine) embrace any *Iurie* or *Inquest*, he shall lose ten times so much as he received; and if he have not whereof to answer so much, then he shall endure a whole yeeres imprisonment: [*203] But if hee shall *embrace* a *Iurie*, without taking any thing for his labour, yet by the *Statute* (*32. H. 8. cap. 9.*) he shall pay ten pounds for every such his *offence.*

Offences in the making of Pannels.

And now, even as those that strive to doe wrong, can little prevaile by running the course of *Law*, though they be mightie to *maintaine*, though they be never so furnished with *Reteyners* and *Followers*, and though they can perswasively deale with *Iurers*, and *Inquests* also, unlesse withall, by the helpe of

---

[93] our Maintenance] other maintenances *WF.*

the *Sheriffe* (or his *Clarke*) such men be *returned*, and put into the *Pannell* for them, as they themselves should nominate, or like: Even so, those *Statutes*, seeing that *Causes* in *Law* depend no lesse upon the sound [*204] and upright *service* of the *Sheriffes*,[94] than doth the *doore* upon the *hookes*, (by the meane of which it openeth and closeth at pleasure) they have in the first place noted two severall *misdemeanours* of that *Officer*, and have referred the *correction* of the same to this *Honourable Assembly* in the *Star-Chamber;* The one, is the untrue demeaning of the *Sheriffe*, in making *Pannels;* the other, is his *falshood* in other *returnes*.

By the *Pannell* is meant that *Catalogue* (or *Roll*) wherein the names of 24. good and lawfull men ought to be *returned* by the *Sheriffe*, out of which the number of *twelve* are to bee *tryed* and *sworne*, and to yeeld their *Verdict* upon each *matter* in *issue*, that is triable (by *Iurie*) between man and man; and the same, or a greater number of them, to be charged for *enquirie* on the behalfe of the *Queene*. In which part, if [*205] the *Sheriffe* shall apply himselfe to *serve*, not the *Court*, and *Iustice*, (whose *minister* hee is) but the one or the other *partie* (that shall *corruptly* winne him) then shall not the better *Cause*, but the fuller *Purse* prevaile; and it shall be all one, whether the *partie* be *Iudge* of his owne *matter*, or *procure* such as himselfe shall *denominate*, to passe upon the *Tryall* for him.

And as in this part of his *Office*, the good *demeanour* of the *Sheriffe* maketh much to the furtherance of *Right;* and his *corrupt* dealing may highly advance *Injurie*, and *Wrong:* So also, by all other the *Returnes* and *Answeres* of his *service* to her *Majesties* Courts, hee may greatly *helpe* or *hurt* the *matter* in question; eyther winning time against the *Plaintiffe*, by dilatorie *Returnes* of his *Writs*, and *Proces;* or wringing the

---

[94] Sheriffes] Sherife *WF*.

Defendant, [*206] by untrue *answer* made of that which he hath in charge, or abusing both them and the *Court,* by sending in no *returne* at all.

In all or the most of which *Cases,* although the partie (defrauded by him) may sometimes helpe himselfe by *averrement* against his *returne;* sometimes, by *complaint* to the *Court* where the *suit* dependeth; and other times may finde *amends,* by an *action* upon the *Case* for his abuse; yet the *Law* seeing that *Iustice* is many times both *delayed* & *deluded* by such unfaithfull *services,* hath first (touching *Pannels* generally) provided by the *Statutes* (42. *Ed.* 3. *cap.* 11.[95] 34. *Edward.* 3. *cap.* 4.[96]) for the better direction of the *Sheriffe* in that behalfe, that (upon paine to be *fined* after the quantitie[97] of the *damage* sustained by the partie) in all manner of *Pannells,* those persons should be put that be most [*207] *substantiall,* worthy of *faith,* and not *suspected,* nor *procured,* but having best knowledge of the *truth,* and being most nigh to the *place,* where the *question* in *Law* doth arise. And (18. *H.* 6. *cap.* 14.) it was ordained to continue for a time,

> That if the *Sheriffe,* or *Bailiffe,* should take any thing for arraying of *Pannels,* the Partie grieved should have his *Action,* and recover ten times so much against him.

And that this abuse may bee the more surely repressed (especially in case where the *service* concerned the *Prince* himselfe) order was taken by the *Statute* (3. *H.* 8. *cap.* 12.)

> That the *Iustices* of *Goale-deliverie,* and of the *Peace,* might reforme all *Pannels* returned before them, to serve the *King;* and that the *Sheriffe* and his *Ministers* should

---

[95] cap. 11.] 28. E. 1: *WF.*
[96] 4.] 4. et ca. 11: *WF.*
[97] the quantitie] *WF;* the quantitie of the trespasse against the King, and to loose the quantitie *MSS of all earlier versions of the treatise.*

> (under the pain of twenty pound) eftsoones returne [*208] the same so reformed by them.

Many other *Rules* there are, particularly set downe by sundrie *Statutes*, concerning the value in lands or goods, of the *Iurors returned*, in sundrie sorts of *Actions;* concerning *Hundredors*, to be inserted in the *Pannell* amongst them; touching the quantitie of the *Issues* that the *Sheriffe* ought to *returne* upon every of their heads, and such other matters, whereof many doe carrie their speciall *paines* within them: all which are over-long to be recited here, and be sufficient of themselves to make the *Body* of a large *Discourse.*

Untrue Returnes by Sheriffes.

To come to the other part thereof, where either the *Sheriffe* will not receive the *Writ* at all, or [*209] (receiving it) will either make no *returne;* or a *subtill* or *false returne* of the same; there is a large *Statute* made, (13. *Ed.* 1. 39.) by which it is enacted,

> That the *partie* may deliver his *Writ* openly to the *Sheriffe*, to be *served*, taking a *Bill* thereof from the *Sheriffe* himselfe, or other *witnesses:* And if hee doe not then *returne* the same, the *partie* shall have *Damages* against him, according to the *perill* that might come unto him by that delay.

The like *Remedie* is there given, if the *Sheriffe* will untruly *returne*, That the *Writ* came so late to his hands, that he could not, for want of time, make *execution* of it. There is *helpe* also for the untrue *returnes* of *small Issues*, upon a man whose Land is able to answere *great:* And for the unjust charging of *Bayliffes* of *Liberties*, to have made him none *answere* of [*210] the *Writs* that he sent unto them: In all which *Cases* of *false returne*, *power* is given to the ordinarie *Iustices*, to *punish* a[98] *Sheriffe* once or twice for his *offences:* But if he *offend*[99] the third time, that then no man shall have to doe therewith, but the *King:* Even as (by the same *Statute*)

> no *Iudge* or *Officer* may take upon him to *punish* a great man (that shall resist the *Sheriffe* in the *execution* of the K. *Writs*) but the King himselfe, to whom that *power* is reserved: Because (*as the* Statute *speaketh*) such *persons* be disturbers of the Kings *Peace*, and of his *Realme.*

But, for as much as the *Under-Sheriffes* (or *Clarkes* of the *Under-Sheriffes*[1]) waxed bold to commit the same *offences,* for which their *Masters* were to be *punished*, and for which, as yet, there was not[2] any *Sword* of *Law* drawne against themselves; [*211] there was (in the time of the same King) an *Ordinance* made, (and called, *Tractatus contra Vice-comites, & Clericos*) By which it is to be[3] provided,

> That if the *Offence* of a *false returne* be found in the *person* of such a *Clarke* to the *Sheriffe;* then shall that *Clarke* both make *Fine* to the *King*, and *satisfie* the *partie* hurt, (if he be able) and the *Sheriffe* to goe quit: But if the *Clarke* be insufficient, then is the *Sheriffe* himselfe to answer for him.

Howbeit, this last *Age* hath proceeded further, and hath given order, (27. *Eliz. cap.* 12.)

> That as well the *Under-Sheriffe*, and his *Clarke* (or *Deputie*) as each *Bayliffe* of *Franchise*, shall take an *Oath*, for the avoiding of this and other corruptions.

It would prove tedious, to prosecute the varietie of all those *paines* [*212] and *forfeitures*, that *Law* (in *force*) hath de-

---

98 a] the *WF.*
99 offend] fall *WF.*
1 Under-Sheriffes] Sheryfes *WF.*
2 which, as yet, there was not] which there was not yet *WF.*
3 is to be] is *WF.*

vised against the untrue *Returnes* of the *Sheriffes*; neither is it so fit for the purpose, that I have now in hand; seeing, that in the most of them, the ordinarie *remedie* (given by those *Statutes*) is sufficient for *revenge:* And therefore, having already opened that *part* which best serveth for giving *Iurisdiction* to this *Court*, I will goe forward to the handling of the rest.

Taking of Money by Iurors.

It is justly to be suspected, that if the *Iurie* take *Money*, to give their *Verdict;* they,[4] with *Iudas*, betray the *truth:* And if it be most true, that *Gifts* and *Bribes* will pervert the *Iudgement*, even of the wisest; then how can it be otherwise, but that the common *man* shall be drawne aside, and corrupted thereby: The [*213] which *fault* is so much the greater, than either is *Conspiracie* or[5] *Maintenance* in the *parties*, (that be but private men) or false and undue dealings in the *Sheriffe*, and his *Clarke*, (being publike *Officers*) as howsoever they should *conclude*[6] amongst themselves, and *close* together: Yet an upright and faithfull *Iurie*, that (without respect of *reward*) would attend the *truth* of their *Evidence*, might overthrow the *frame* of whatsoever *mischiefe* they should imagine, or intend betweene them: And therefore, when the *Iurours* also, that be (as I said) more than halfe *Iudges* of the *Controversie;* shall *pledge* the one of the parties in that *Cup* of *Poyson*, which hee hath *brewed*, to destroy the *life* of his adversaries *right;* what can be looked for, but that the better *Side* shall have the worse, and take the *fall?*

[*214] And this being seene to the *Law*, it was ordained, 34. *Ed.* 3. *c.* 8.[7]

---

[4] they] they will *WF.*
[5] or] and *WF.*
[6] conclude] collude *WF.*
[7] 34. Ed. 3. c. 8.] 38. E. 3. ca. 13. *WF.*

That if a *Iuror* (in any *Enquest* to be taken for the *King*, or betweene *parties*) doe take any thing, by himselfe, or by any other of the *parties*, *Plaintiffe* or[8] *Defendant*, to say the *Verdict;* then shal he pay *Decies tantum*, ten times so much as he hath taken; whereof the one halfe be to the *King*, (whose *Iustice* and *Iudgement* hee hath perverted) and the other halfe to the *partie* (or any other) that wil *sue* for the same: And if he have not to satisfie the *Law*, then to have the *imprisonment* of a whole yeare.

In which *Statute*, one thing is specially to be observed; That, to *take* anything whatsoever (for *saving* of the *Verdict*) is an *offence* against it: although the *Statute*, (3. *H*. 7.) that submitteth this *fault* to the *punishment* [*215] of the *Star-chamber*, hath no mention, but of the *taking* of *Money* onely: Which words, if they be not *construed* by an *equitie*, the whole *Law* may (for this *point*) be deluded[9] by it.

Riots, Routs, and Rebellious Assemblies.

After this, and the rest of the *offences*, that are carried in the *Lap* of *Fraud*, *Covin*, and *Deceit;* great *Riots*, and *unlawfull Assemblies*, that will make their *way* by *fine force*, came next to my hand: The which two, though they be distinct *faults*, both in the propertie of their owne *nature*, and in the *order* of these *Statutes;* yet, because (for the most part) the one is but the *effect*, and *sequele* of the other, I will *wynde* them up both in one *Bottome* together.

[*216] Not with[10] cause, but for distinction sake, doth this *Statute* (3. *Henr*. 7.) call some *Riots*, great: For sundrie former *Lawes* doe note two manner of *Riots;* the one *lesse*, aswell in respect of the small number of the *persons* that commit it, as in regard of the small *terrour*, *disturbance* or *hurt* that en-

---

[8] other of the parties, Plaintiffe or] other, of the partie plaintyfe, or *WF*.

[9] deluded] eluded *WF*.

[10] with] without *WF*.

sueth of it; the other *great*, or *hainous*, because it savoureth of a more general *disobedience*, even to the shaking of the *Estate;* and is, or may be (in regard of the number or quarrell) a very *Seed* of *Mutinie*, and *Rebellion.*

And therefore the *Statutes* (5. *Richard* 2. *cap.* 6. *&* 7. *Richard* 2. *cap.* 2. *&* 6.) doe terme the *Riots* of this latter sort by the names of *Rumours*, great *Ridings*, *Routs*, and *Riots*, against the *Peace*. The *Statute* (2. *Henr.* 5. *cap.* 9.) calleth them *Assemblies* of *people* in great [*217] *number*, in manner of *insurrection;* and the *Lawes* (5. *Rich.* 2. *cap.* 6.[11] *&* 1. *Mar. Parl.* 1. *cap.* 12.) doe name them *Rebellious Insurrections*, and *Rebellious Assemblies.*

But the *offences* of all these sorts, are now at this day distinguished by three received names; that is, *unlawfull Assemblie*, *Rout*, and *Riot.*

An *unlawfull Assemblie*, is commonly taken to be, where a *companie* of three *persons* (or moe) bee gathered together; to the end, to commit (forcible[12]) an *unlawfull Act.*

A *Rout*, is likewise construed to be, where such a *Companie* of three (or more) being gathered to such an *end*, doe move *forward* (by *going* or *riding*) for the putting of their *intention* in practice; and yet doe not come to the very *actuall* handling and execution of their *purpose.*

[*218] A *Riot* is the very *effect*, and *finall act* of such a *Company* of three (or moe) *assembling*, *proceeding*, and *putting in execution* (forcibly) that *unlawfull worke* which they intended.

As for example, If three *persons* (or moe) under the number of *twelve*, doe *assemble* themselves *unlawfully*, to beat any *person;* or to enter forcibly into the *house* or *land* of any[13] other, or to pull down the *inclosures*, or[14] any *Parke*, *Warren*,

---

[11] cap. 6.] ca. 2. *WF.*
[12] forcible] forciblie *WF.*
[13] any] an *WF.*
[14] or] of *WF.*

or *ground inclosed;* or to destroy any *Fish-pond*, *Poole*, or *Dove-house*, or to do such other *act*, and (being so *assembled*) doe goe forward about the same, and doe effect their desire; then is this an *unlawfull Assembly*, for their first *meeting;* a *Rout*, for their *moving forward;* and a *Riot*, in the *end*, by their *execution.*

The word *Rout*, came from the *Saxons* (our *elders*) who to this day [*219] call *Rot*, a *band* (or *companie* of *men*) riding together.

Riot, we borrowed of the *French*, *Rioter*, which is, to braule, or scold, because most commonly *outragious deeds* doe follow *contentious* and *scolding words.*

The *evils* that will ensue, if fellow subjects may be suffered to run (when they list) on heapes, and to put and push each at other (as the wild and savage Beasts of the *field* and *Forrest* are wont to doe) be so great and apparant, that they bewray themselves, and need no words to *blaze* them: The *paines* thereof that *Law* hath inflicted upon such *Assemblies*, *Routs*, and *Riots*, bee these: They shall be taken by the *Iustices* of the *Peace*, and *Sheriffe*, and bee throwne into the next *Goale*, till they have made *Fine*, and *Ransome* to the King, 15. *Rich.* 2. *cap.* 2.

[*220] *Rioters*, attainted of great and hainous *Riots*, shall be *imprisoned* one whole yeare (at the least) without *Baile*, or *Mainprise*, and then make grievous *Fines:* And such as shall bee attainted of *Petite Riots*, shall have *imprisonment*, and make *Fine*, as shall seeme good to the Kings *Iustices*, 2. *Henr.* 5. *cap.* 8.

But if the *number* of such an *Assemblie* be *twelve*, or above, that shall attempt any of the things prohibited by the *Statute*, (made against *unlawfull* and *rebellious Assemblies*, in the first yeere of Queene *Maries* Reigne) and doe continue together by the space of one *houre*, after *proclamation* orderly made for them to depart; then is their *offence Felonie*, and may receive *punishment* in another *degree*, and in another *Court*, by the ordinarie course of lawfull *tryall.*

[*221] Thus have I detected these severall[15] *Offences*, that are specially signified by these two *Statutes:* Wherein I have not so largely extended my *Discourse*, as the *Argument* it selfe will beare; (especially for that part which describeth the *Paines*) partly, because I undertooke to make onely a *Summarie* shew of the whole *Matter;* and partly, for that those Honourable *Iudges* are not tyed (as I said) to the prescript *Paines* of those *Statutes:* but may (as the *Case* shall offer to their grave Considerations) eyther *alter*, *encrease*, or otherwise *qualifie* any of the same.

[*222] COUNTERFEITS OF PRIVIE TOKENS.

To these (for an end) I must adjoyne such other *Statutes* also (now in force) as have been enacted since that time; and in which, there is speciall *direction* of *power* given to the *Lords* and other of her Majesties *Councell* in the *Star-chamber*, as namely first that *Act* (made 33. *Henr.* 8. *cap.* 1.) against the *Counterfeitors* of *Privie Tokens*, and *Letters*, in the names of other *persons*, for the obteyning of *money*, or other *goods.* Then that other *Act* (which passed 4. & 5. *Phil.* & *Mar. cap.* 8.) against the conveighing away of *Maidens* under the age of sixteene yeeres, from the possession of their *Parents*, or *Governours;* and against the *contracting* of *Matrimonie* with any such *Maidens*, their *Parents* not knowing thereof, or [*223] not *consenting* thereunto. And lastly, that *Act* (ordained in the 5. yere of our Soveraigne *Lady* that now is, *cap.* 14.) (†)

(†) 5. *Eliz. c.* 14.

---

[15] severall] eight severall *WF.*

against the *forging* of *deeds*, *Instruments*, and *Writings*, in their sundry *Natures* and *Degrees*. Of which *Lawes*, I shall not need to spend any further *speech*, but onely thus to point them out; considering that they doe most amplie and plainely comprehend within themselves, aswell the severall *natures* of the *faults*, and the *evils* that ensue thereof, as also the *punishments* that are to be inflicted for everie of the same.

And[16] therefore, this is all that (for this *time* and *service*) I purposed to say of this most noble and praise-worthy *Court;* the beames of whose bright *Iustice*, (equall in beautie with *Hesperus* and *Lucifer*, as *Aristotle* said in a like case) doe *blaze* and *spread* themselves as *farre* [*224] as this *Realme* is *long*, or *wide:* and by the *influence* of whose *super-eminent Authoritie*, all other *Courts* of *Law*, and *Iustice*, that wee have, are both the more surely *supported*, and the more evenly *kept*, and *managed*.

The Court of Requests.[17]

In that the Court of *Requests* handleth *Causes*, that desireth[18] *Moderation* of the *rigour* which the *Common Law* denounceth, it doth plainely participate with the nature of the *Chancerie;* but in that the *Bills* here be exhibited to the *Majestie* of the *King* onely, and to none other; and in that the *Masters*[19] of *Requests* were[20] sworne of the *Kings Councell*, and the *Place*[19] hath continually been served with a *Clarke*, that was ever therewithall one of the *Clarks* of the *Kings Privie* [*225] *Seale*, which[21] is yet still the originall *Writ* of

---

[16] *Both F and H here resume, having omitted the preceding forty-one pages.*

[17] Requests] *F BT;* the Requests *H (and similarly twice on the next lines, BT there agreeing with H). F places this section on the Court of Requests after the sections on the Warden's and Duchy Courts, which appear later here and in H. For the other changes in order in F in these next pages, see the table below, Appendix, pp. 148-149.*

[18] desireth] *F;* desire *H.*

[19] the Masters . . . Place] *H;* it *F.*

[20] were] be *H.*

[21] which . . . Court] *H; om. F.*

this *Court:*[21] It seemeth to communicate with the *Star-chamber* it selfe, and to derive her *Authoritie* immediately from the *Royall Person*, and his *Councell*,[22] as that doth.

For the very same *Authorities*, and[23] *Reasons*, by the which wee have alreadie proved before, that the *King* may be appealed unto, for matter of *Crime*, where just cause doth enforce it; doe no lesse forcibly convince, that he is also to be fled unto for *Equitie*, in rare cases in civill *suit*, where the ordinarie rule of his *Law* is too hard and heavie for his subjects.

And no lesse incident is it to the Kingly *Office*, to relieve the *Suitors* oppressed under the burthen of grievous *Law*, than to devise *correction* for the insolent *Malefactors*, against whom no former [*226] *Law* or *Statute* hath beene provided.

It is out of all doubt therefore, that as our *Kings* have used personally to receive *complaints* of *Criminall* condition, and have *adjudged* thereof, by themselves, or by their *Councel* of *Estate;* so haue they also, from time to time, taken knowledge of *Civil suites* (especially offered by the poorer sort of *Subjects*, or by their own *houshold men;*) & have for the most part recommended the same to the care of some of their said *Councell*, assisted with the advice, of men learned both in the *Civill* and *Common Lawes:* so as some one temporall *Lord*, or *Bishop*, two Doctors, and two *Common Lawyers* have beene many times knowne to have sitten here for the *Requests* together.

And hereof[24] it was (as I suppose) that the *Cause* of the two [*227] Sisters, (whereof I have told you in the *Star-chamber* before) was said to have beene heard before the *President* of the *Requests*, that is, before the *Lord*, or *Bishop*, which was the principall person of this *Commission* or[25] *Company*.

Now, albeit there can no other beginning hereof bee con-

---

22 and his Councell,] *om. F H.*
23 Authorities, and] *H; om. F.*
24 hereof] *H;* therfore *F.*
25 Commission or] *om. F;* Bench or *H.*

ceived, then together with the very *regality*, and *kingdome* it selfe; yet forasmuch as they of this *Court* have not alwayes had their standing *place* of *resort*, but have untill the *age* next before this, *remained*, and *remooved* with the *King* wherso-ever he went, travailing betweene the *Prince*, and *petitioners*, by direction from the mouth of the King: I have in this, as in the *Star-chamber* also, taken the first apparent setling and manifest *continuance* thereof, for the very *spring* and *originall* it selfe.

[*228] And I have lately seene, that from the eighth yeare of King *Henry* the seventh, ever since which time this *Court* hath rested in the place called the *White-hall;* the *bookes* of the *acts* (or *Entries*) there have been orderly digested and kept, in which you may reade the *handling* of the *causes*, not onely of *poore men*, and the *Kings servants*, but also of sundry noble *Persons*,[26] *Abbots*, *Knights*, *Esquires*, and other rich & wealthy *complainants*. Howbeit I doe well *remember*, that within these 40. *yeares*, the *bills* of *complaints presented* there, did ordinarily carry the one, or the other of these two *sugges-tions*, namely, that the *Plaintiffe* was a very poore man, not able to *sue* at the *Common Law*, or the Kings *servants*,[27] ordi-narily *attendant* upon his *person*, or in his *houshold*. But be-cause *enlargement* of *jurisdiction* is not proper to *Court*[28] [*229] alone, but common to it with all the rest, I will not now stand to object it,[29] but hasten to an end.

The Masters of the *Requests* are neither called by *Writ*, nor appointed by *Commission*, nor created by *Patent* as other[30] *Iudges* be; which argue the immediate *authority* of the Prince to bee exercised by them;[30] but onely have[31] *Letters Patent* for their *Fees* and *Sallarie*, and were wont to[32] take the same

---

[26] noble Persons,] *om. F H.*
[27] servants] *F;* servant *H.*
[28] Court] *F;* this Court *H.*
[29] it] *F;* against it *H.*
[30] as other . . . them] *H; om. F.*
[31] onely have] *F;* they have onely *H.*
[32] were wont to] doe *F H.*

Oath,[33] which the *Councellors* of *estate*[34] doe yet[35] conceive.

The *Clarkeship* of this Court hath, as I said, beyond all memory beene committed to a *Clarke* of the *Privie Seale.*

For Master *Richard Offley,*[36] now *Clarke,* hath served in that place sixe and forty yeares, succeeding therein to his Uncle *Richard Turner,* who had spent threescore and sixe yeares partly as servant, and [*230] partly as Officer there. The same *Turner* had followed *Robert Sampson,* the successor of *Lacy,* both well knowne unto him, all which were in their times ioyntly both *Clarkes* of the *Privy Seale,* and of this Court also.

The *Atturneyes* were in my first knowledge of them,[37] but two onely; and now are three, whose places are at the disposition of the *Clarke.*

The usuall Processe is by *Privy Seale,* alias *Privie Seale, Attachment,* and *Writ* of *Rebellion,* if the contumacy of the Defendant doe so deserve: In the rest of the proceedings, the course is not much different from the order of the *Chancery.*

[*231] THE PRESIDENT AND COUNCELLS.[38]

King *Hen.* 8. established one Court of *President* and *Councell* in the *Marches* of *Wales,* and another like Court of *President* and *Councell* in the North parts, both which be Courts of *Equitie* in the[39] principall jurisdiction, although they doe withall, exercise other powers by vertue of other severall *Commissions,* and doe[40] accompany the same.

THE DUTCHY COURT[41] OF LANCASTER.

The Court of the *Dutchy* or *Countie Palatine* of *Lancaster,*

---

33 Oath] *F;* oath in effect *H.*
34 of estate] *H; om. F.*
35 yet] *om. F H.*
36 Offley] Osley *F H.*
37 of them] *F; om. H.*
38 President and Councells] Presidents and Counsells *H;* President and Councell in the Marches of Wales *F;* Courtes of President and Connseils *BT.*
39 the] *F;* their *H BT.*
40 and doe] *F;* that doe *H BT.*
41 Court] *F BT; om. H.*

grew out of the grant of the same[42] King *Ed.* 3 who first gave that *Dutchie* to his Sonne *Iohn* of *Gaunt*, and endowed it with such Royall *rights* as the *Countie Palatine* of *Chester* [*232] had. And forasmuch as it was afterwards extincted in the person of *K. H.* 4. by reason of the Union of it with the *Crowne* of the *Realme*, the same *K.* knowing himselfe to be more rightfully *Duke* of *Lancaster*, than *King* of *England*, determined to save his right in the *Dutchie*, whatsoever should befall him in the possession of the *Kingdome.* And therefore he separated his *Dutchie* from the *Crowne*, and setled it so, in the naturall person of *himselfe*, and his *heires*, as if he had beene no *K.* or politicke body at all: In which plight it continued during the Reignes of *K. H.* 5. and *K. Hen.* 6. that were his descendants.

But when *K. Ed.* 4. had by recovery of the *Crowne*, continued the right of the House of *Yorke*, he feared not to appropriate that *Dutchie* to the *Crowne* againe.[43] And in this manner it came together with the [*233] *Crowne* to *K. H.* 7. who liking well of the policie of *K. E.* 4[44] by whose right also he obtained the *Kingdom*, made like separation of the *Dutchie* as he had done before, and so left[45] to his *posteritie* which doe yet enjoy it.

The Court of Wards and Liveries.

The Court of *Wards* began in our memorie, about 32.[46] yeare of the Raigne of *K. H.* 8. who also in the next yeare after added thereunto the office of the *Master* of the *Liveries*, and therewithall conjoyned their[47] names, ordayning that it should bee called the Court of *Wards*[48] and *Liveries.*

---

[42] the same] *F; om. H BT.*

[43] againe] *F H;* againe, and yet so, that he suffered the Courte and officers to remaine as he founde them *BT.*

[44] K. E. 4.] King Hen. 4 *F H BT.*

[45] so left] left *F;* soe left it *H BT.*

[46] 32.] the 32. *F H BT.*

[47] their] *F;* the *H BT.*

[48] Wards] *F;* his Wards *H BT.*

The Court of Augmentation.[49]

The same *King* likewise had erected one Court of the generall [*234] Surveyors of his Lands, and one other of the *augmentations* and *revenues* of his *Crowne*, and a third Court of the *first fruits* and *tenths* of *Benefices*. But all these were afterwards dissolved, and by *Queene Mary* united to the Court of *Exchequer*.

The Wardens Court.[50]

Howsoever in the stormes of *open warre* and *hostilitie* between us and the *Scots*, our most *ancient enemies*, the *subjects* on either side have gone to wracke, and the *Lawes* have beene silent, while the Drum and Trumpet were heard to sound, yet in every calme, and upon everie truce, or peace taken and concluded, both Humanitie, Reason,[51] and Custome have afforded mutuall, and reciprocall deliverie of *Law*, and *Iustice* to the one subject against [*235] the other: without the which, truce[52] were not onely no truce at all, but the continuance of a daily, & most dangerous lying in wait, which would bring with it a greater evill and mischiefe, then *warre* it selfe.

And therfore to the end that the conditions of the *peace* agreed upon, might be inviolably observed for the time, and that, both restitution for *harmes*, and punishments[53] upon *harme doers*, might be made, and executed with all indifferencie: Certaine Courts have of long time beene *maintained* by the *Wardens*, or *Keepers* of the *Marches*, and *Limitative*[54] grounds, that doe border upon either of the said *Kingdomes*, the which are open to all that will complaine of any *Offence*,

---

[49] Augmentation] *F;* Augmentacions, etc. *H;* Surveyors, Augmentacions, and first fruites *BT*.

[50] Court] *H;* Court in the Marches of Scotland *F*.

[51] Humanitie, Reason] *H;* humane reason *F*.

[52] truce] *F;* the truce *H*.

[53] punishments] punishment *F H*.

[54] Limitative] Limytaine *F;* lymitary *H*.

tending to the *violation* of that *Common peace* of both the *Nations.*

And albeit that is very *probable,* [*236] that the same begun with the first truce taken betweene us, and the *Scots,* (seeing that without it, or some such mean,[55] the Articles of the *truce* could not well bee maintained): yet forasmuch as the bounds betweene us and the *Scots,* were not constant nor setled, but verie moveable and uncertaine, (even as either side did for the time winne, or lose upon the other,) untill that both the Townes of *Carlile* and *Barwick* (being meetest to command at either end) were without *change,* reduced to our hands and possession.

I suppose, that these Courts were planted about the time of King *Edw.* 2.(†) or the 3.[56] and so taking root from thence by little and little, to have growne to that stayed order and authoritie which now they doe enjoy. They on our part, be at this day in number 3. whereof one hath sprung up since the [*237] time of *K. H.* 6. who in a *Statute* (made in the 31. yeare of his reign, for redresse of *Indictments* taken there) reciteth onely the two *courts* of the *East* and *West Marches,* using no words at al of the *Middle March,* which is now of the like credit with them.

The same *Statute* also boundeth the *Iurisdiction* of these Courts, not to extend beyond the *Shires* of *Westmerland, Cumberland,* and *Northumberland,* and the Towne of *Newcastle* upon the River of *Tyne.*

What manner of proceeding they use, I do not throughly know, neither is it greatly pertinent to this present labour, and therefore leaving the search thereof to such as shall bee

(†) *Edmund Comes Arundel, fuit custos Marchiae Scotiae 6. E. 2. pillis exitus.*

---

[55] such mean] other meane *F;* such meanes *H.* *F also lacks the supporting marginal citation.*

[56] Edw. 2. or the 3.] *H;* Edw. 3 *F.*

desirous to understand the same, I will proceede as I have begun.

[*238] THE PARLIAMENT.[57]

But now the *Ecclesiasticall* Courts being numbred, and these meer[58] *Lay-Courts* thus handled, it resteth, that I adjoyn the *Parliament*, which is mixed of both these natures, as having the *Bishops* in respect of their *Baronies*, and not of their *Churches*, joyned with the *Lay-Lords* to make up the second *estate* thereof. The first *estate* consisting of the *Prince* alone, and the third of the *Comminaltie*, without any of the *Clergie* at all.

Besides the which, it is summoned to devise *Lawes*, both *Ecclesiasticall*, *Civill*, *Criminall*, and *Martiall*, it ministreth the matter whereupon all the rest of the Courts do worke, and it hath in sóme cases, an ordinarie *Iurisdiction* also.

That which wee (now agreeing [*239] with the *Scots*) doe name a *Parliament*, the *Frenchmen* doe call *Les Estates*, or *Assembly des Estates*, because with them there, as with us also, the *Estates* of the *Land* doe meete thereat, to *consult;* and the same in *Germany*, is termed a *Dyet*, for these other Courts that carry the name of *Parliament* in *France*, be but ordinarie Courts of *Iustice*, which as *Paulus Iovius* writeth, are thought to have bin planted there by us. And of which our owne *Councells* (established in *Wales*, and in the *North-parts*) doe beare the neerest shew, and resemblance.

THE WORD PARLIAMENT.[59]

The word *Parliament* (saith one) is compounded of *Parium* and *Lamentum*, because (as he thinketh) the *Peeres* of the *Countrie* did at these meetings *lament* and *complain* [*240]

---

[57] The Parliament] *BT;* Parliament *F; om. H. BT actually places this two paragraphs later.*

[58] these meer] *H;* those *F.*

[59] The word Parliament] *F; om. H;* Parlement divided *BT.*

each to other of the enormities of their *Countrey*, and thereupon provided redresse for the same.

But their opinion is more probable, as I thinke, which derive *Parliament* simply from the *French word Parler*, and that also from the *Greeke* word Παϱαλαλειν, both signifying to *speake*, and so by adding the *termination Ment*, which is common in the *French tongue* as well to *nownes*[60] as *adverbs*, doe make up *Parliament*, meaning thereby an *assembly* of *men* called together, to *speake* or *conferre* their advices, or opinions. And so also it may not unfitly bee called *Parliament*, for that each man there doth, or should *Parler la ment*, speak his mind: But *Laurence Valla* mis-liketh that manner of *Etymologie*, and therefore I will not stand upon it.

I dare not take upon me to set downe the very time in which the *word Parliament* came first in use; [*241] but forasmuch as it was *transported* out of *France*, it is not *unprobable* to *guesse*, that it began here shortly after the *time* of the *Norman Conquest*.

One of the first *authenticall* reports of that name *Parliament*, that I have found, is in the *Statute* made the 3. of *Edw.* 1. and commonly called *Westminster* the *first;* where, that *Assemblie* is said to be, *Le Primer Parliament generall apres Coronement le Roy*. But yet that is not the very first use of the word; for in the Statute called *Articuli Cleri*, and published the 9. of[61] *Edw.* 2. these words are read amongst others; *Temporibus progenitorum nostrorum quondam Regum Angliae in diversis Parliamentis suis, &c.* Which words, *progenitorum* and *quondam*, must needs reach higher than to *Edward* the first, that was but father to him that spake it. So that I can willingly herein *subscribe* to the *opinion* of *Polydore Virgil*, [*242] who in the 11. Booke of his *English Historie*, which

---

[60] nownes] *F;* manie nownes *H BT.*

[61] the 9. of] the 9. *F;* 9. *H BT.*

containeth the reigne of K. *Henry* the first, that was sonne to the *Conquerour*, writing of the great Assembly at *Salisburie*, saith thus; *At illud opposite habeo dicere, Reges ante haec tempora non consuevisse populi conventum consultandi causa (nisi perraro) facere, adeo ut ab Henrico id institutum Iure manasse dici possit, &c.* And a little after, *More Gallico vulgo Parliamentum appellant, &c.* And this is so much the more credible, as that King laboured by all meanes, and especially by the restitution of the ancient *Lawes*, (as all *Historians* doe agree) to heale the hearts of the *Englishmen*, which were before deepely wounded by the *oppression* of his Father, and Brother *William;* to the end, that he might thereby the better keepe the Crowne of this Realme against the[62] elder Brother *Robert*, who had both colour of good [*243] right, and had mooved his claime thereto.

But at what time soever, after the *Conquest*, this Court began to be called by the name of *Parliament;* this is certaine, that was[63] before knowne to the *Saxons*, or *Englishmen:* sometimes, by the word *Synoth*, and *Micle; Synoth*, of the *Greeke* Συνόδος, now appropriated to the[64] *Ecclesiasticall Meetings* onely: And sometimes by these tearmes, *Micel-Gemot*, *Witena-Gemot*, & *Ealrawitena-Gemot;* that is to say, the *great Meeting*, the *Meeting of the Wise-men*, or, the *Meeting of all the Wise-men:* For *Witen* signifieth *Wise-men; Ealra, all;* and *Gemot*, a *Meeting:* of which last word, the names of *Shire-moote*, and *Folke-moote*, and *Haly-moote;* that is to say, the *Assembly*, or *Meeting* of the *men* of the *Shire*, of the *men* of a *Towne*, and of the *Tenants* of a *Hall*, or *Mannour*, had their beginnings [*244] also. And as *Synoth* is more used in the *Acts* of *Parliaments* themselves, so *Gemot* is more familiar to the *Historians*.

---

[62] the] *F;* his *H BT.*

[63] was] the same was *F H BT.*

[64] the] *F; om. H BT.*

Thus much as well of the *present*, as of the *ancient* usuall *Name:* Now let us looke into the thing it selfe.

The conformitie and reason[65] of the three Estates in Parliament.

Like as in *Warre*, where the *King* is present in Person; and with him, the *Nobilitie*, *Gentrie*, and *Yeomanrie;* there is the *force* and *puissance* of the *Realme:* Even so in *Peace*, wheresoever the *Prince* is, as the *Head*, to give *life*, (that is to say) to yeeld the highest and last *assent;* And where the *Baronie*, consisting of the *Lords Spirituall*, and *Temporall;* and the *Comminaltie*, made up of the *Knights*, and *Burgesses*, be as the *Bodie*, [*245] present at his *Call*, to the end, to *deliberate*, *conferre*, and *conclude;* there is also the *Councell*, and *Policie* of the *Realme:* So that, for as much as every man, from the highest to the lowest, is there either in person, or by procuration; therefore of right *reason*, every man is said to be bound by that which doth passe from such an *Assembly*. And this frame of *Policie* is both *naturall*, and *harmonicall: Naturall*, in that it hath an imitation of the naturall bodie of man, truly called a *little World;* out of the three *Cells* whereof, namely, the *Head*, *Breast*, and *Belly*, the whole three *powers* of the *Soule* doe open, and utter themselves: and *Harmonicall*, because from such, and so well-tuned[66] a *Base*, *Meane*, and *Treble*, there proceedeth a most exquisite *consent*, and delicious *melodie*.

[*246] The beginning of the Parliament.

The beginning of which manner of *Consultation*, and namely with us of this Realme, I see not how I can derive it from any other time, than from that, in which the *German* or *English*[67] did set their first foot on this *Land*, to invade it. For *Cornelius*

---

[65] reason] *H BT;* Relation *F.*
[66] well-tuned] tuned *F H BT.*
[67] or English] *F;* (or English) Nation *H BT.*

Tacitus writing of the manners of the ancient *Germans*, sayth thus: *Nec Regibus infinita potestas, de minoribus rebus Principes consultant, de majoribus omnes.*

THE CONTINUANCE OF THE PARLIAMENT, TILL THE CONQUEST.

Neither did they, together with the change of the Soile, make change of this[68] wonted manner of deliberation: For it is yet extant, in *Monuments* left behind them, that [*247] after their comming hither, they frequented the same order in counsailing, which they had used in their owne Countrey before.

For proofe whereof, I might call *Beda*, the *Saxon* Historiographer, to witnesse: who reporting how the *Christian Faith* tooke root by little and little among them, in their particular Kingdomes within this *Land*, writeth, That King *Edwin* of *Northumberland*, would not embrace the Preaching of the *Gospel*, before that he had communed and consulted with his *Friends*, his *Nobilitie*, and his *Wise-men;* and that *Sigebert*, the King of the *East Saxons*,[69] being likewise moved to be *baptized*, did first call a *Councell* of his *Subjects;* and finding them all to favour the *motion*, did then himselfe also assent unto it.

But because the *Synods* or *Parliaments* themselves be most faithfull [*248] witnesses of their owne doings; and for that also the *Kingdome* of the *West Saxons* prevailing over the rest, and melting (as it were) all their Crownes, to make one for her selfe, did in the end become *Mistris* or *Monarch* of the whole *Heptarchie*, or seven *Kingdomes*, into which this *Land* was before divided: I will, for a while, leave *Historians*, and come to the *Synods;* first shewing, by one or two *examples*,

---

[68] this] *F;* this their *H BT*.

[69] the East Saxons] *F;* Eastsex *H BT*.

what *persons* were wont to be present at the *Parliaments* of that *Kingdome;* and then confirming the like to have been used, after such time as the whole *Land* was reduced to one entire *Estate* and *Monarchie.*

Ina, the King of the *West Saxons*,[70] who began his Reigne about the yeare after the *Incarnation* of our *Lord Christ*, 712. began[71] his *Parliament* thus: *Ego*[72] *Inas beneficio Dei Occiduorum Saxonum Rex, &c.*[72]

> I *Ina*, by Gods gift, King of the *West* [*249] *Saxons*, with the advice & teaching of *Cenred* my Father, *Hedde* my Bishop, *Ercenwald*[73] my Bishop, and with all my *Aldermen*, and the eldest *Wise men* of my people (†), and also a great *Assembly* of Gods servants, was carefull concerning the health of our Soules, and establishment of our Kingdome, &c.

The necessitie[74] of the 3. Estates in the making of *Lawes*. One Example[74]

Now let us see if the three *Estates* of *Parliament* (that is to say) the[75] *Nobilitie*, and *Commons*, maybe found here. First, the K. *Name* is expresly added; the *Nobilitie*, is signified under these *Bishops and Aldermen:* for before the *divisions* of the Realms[76] into *Shires*, every large *territorie* had an *Alderman*, or *Governour;* who was, after the *allotment* into *Shires*, for the most part, an *Earle:* in token whereof, almost all our *Earles*, to this day, doe beare the *name* of one *Shire*, or

(†) *Mid eallum mintem Ealdormannum & tham yldestam minre theod.*

---

[70] the West Saxons] *F;* Westsex *H BT.*

[71] began] *F;* beginneth *H BT.*

[72] Ego . . . Rex, &c.] *om. F H BT.*

[73] Ercenwald] *F;* and Ercenwold *H BT.*

[74] The necessitie . . . Example] *om. F H BT.*

[75] the] *F;* the Kinge, the *H BT.*

[76] divisions of the Realms] *F;* division of the Realme *H BT.*

other. The *Comminaltie*, is partly included [*250] in the words; *The eldest Wisemen of my people*, which betokeneth the *Laitie*, and partly in the words, *A great assembly of Gods Servants*, which doe notifie the *Clergie*, called so then, as it may appeare by the very first *Chapter* of the same[77] *Lawes*, for that they were consecrated to *Gods service*.

And lest that any man should think that these *Estates* were called together more for their *advice* and *counsell* to be given to the *King*, than for any *authority* or *interest* they had in making the *Law:* First, the *Preamble* calleth those *Lawes*, *Our Doomes or Iudgements;* and the *Purvieu* saith, *Wee bid or command* in the plurall number, which also may not be restrained to the King alone, for *honours sake*, as we now use to speake; for he is there named, *I Ina* in the singular number onely.

[*251] Thus much I note, once for all, that I be not hereafter troubled to repeat the same things againe.

About one hundred yeeres after the death of this *Ina*, one *Alfred*, a King, not of the *West-Saxons* onely (as he calleth himselfe) but rather both of the *Englishmen* and *Saxons* (as *Asserius* saith, that wrote his *life*) did (as he telleth) in his *Preface* to his *Lawes*, gather together and put in writing certain ordinances made by *Wise men* in sundry *Synods* of sundrie former Kings, as namely *Ina* before-said, *Offa* the King of *Middle England*, and *Ethelbert* of *Kent*, the first *Christned Prince* of all the *Saxon Nation;* which Collection of *Lawes* he also saith, that he shewed to all his own *Wise men*, and they likewise thought them meet to bee observed. (†)

(†) *Ego Aluredus occidentalium Saxonum Rex, prudentissimorum e nostris consilio usus sum, atque in iis omnibus placuit edici eorum observationem.*

---

[77] very first Chapter of the same] *F;* first Chapter of the very same very first Chapter of the very same *H BT.*

But what maketh it to the three Estates, will some men say, that [*252] these Kings and their *Wise men*, which may well seeme to bee but their *privie Counsellors*, did establish *Lawes?* Yes, very much; for here the word *Witena, Wise-men*, doth include the *Nobilitie* and *Commons*, because they be *Counsellors* of the Realme, (for the time) in respect whereof the assembling of them, was of some called *Wytena Gemote, a meeting of the Wise-men*, (as I told you) and of other some it is termed *Commune Concilium Regni*, the *Common Councell* of the *Realme.*

And that this must be so understood in this place, I will use none other Argument than the testimonie of *Alfred* himselfe drawn out of the same place: for he saith (as you have heard) *That the* Lawes *of K.* Ina *were made by a* Synod *of* wise men, and what those *Wise-men* were, you have also understood, by the *report* of K. *Ina* himself, in the style of his [*253] own *Lawes* (that is to say) by the *Nobility* & *Comminalty* besides the *King*.

Another Example.[78]

Furthermore, that I lose not another *advantage* offered me by this *authoritie*, I must also gather thereby, that not onely the *Kingdomes* of *Northumberland*, *Eastsex*, and *Westsex*, used the three estates in making their *Lawes*, but also that they of *Kent*, and *Middle England*, maintained the very same *order:* For King *Alfreds* words (as you see) be one and the same for them all, and then consequently their manner was one and the same through all.

But now, that I may at the length leave these *Heptarchies*, or *petty Kings* and passe to the *Monarchs* and *Great ones*, the same *Alfred* (after that the whole *Nations*[79] had *yeelded*[80]

---

[78] Another Example] *om. F H BT.*

[79] whole Nations] same Nations *F;* whole Nation *H BT.*

[80] yeelded] yeelded themselves *F H BT.*

unto *him*, and were *shrouded* under his *protection* against the *furious stormes* of the *Danish Invasion*) did at one time conclude a *peace* with *Guthrum*, the K. of [*254] the *Danes*, the Style whereof beginneth thus,

> This is the *Peace* which K. *Alfred* and *Guthrum*,[81] and all the *Wise men* of the *English Nation* have taken, &c.

Loe here you see *Ealra wytena Gemote*, An Assemblie of all the *Wise men*.

After him *Edward* called his *Wise men* to *Excester*, and consulted with them for the better observation of the *peace* of[82] his owne *Realme*. And he also at another time, by the advice of the[83] *Wise men*, renued and confirmed the *League* that *Alfred* had taken before with the *Danish Captain*.

King *Athelstan* concludeth his famous *Parliament* holden at *Gratlie*, thus;

> All this was ordained in that great *Synode* at *Gratlie*, at which was the *Arch-Bishop*, *Wolshelme*, with all the *Noble men* and *Wise men* that K. *Ethelstane* gathered together. (†)

And the same King did also afterwards [*255] call another *Assembly* of his *Wise men* to *Excester*, to *consult* for the better *execution* of these former *Ordinances*.

Edmond the King summoned a great *Synode* at *London*, both of the *order* of the *Spiritualtie*, and of the *Temporaltie*, the which in the second part of the *Law* there made, he calleth by one general name his *Witena*, *Wise-men*, and thanketh them[84] for their helpe in that advise.

(†) *Cum eo optimates & sapientes ab Athelstano convocati, &c.*

---

[81] Guthrum] *F;* Kinge Guthrum *H BT.*

[82] of] *F;* in *H BT.*

[83] the] *F;* his *H BT.*

[84] them] them all *F H BT.*

After him King *Edgar* published certaine *Lawes*, which were made (as he saith) by the *Counsell* of his *Wise-men*.

The like Title and conclusion have those *Statutes* also which King *Etheldred* ordained at *Woodstocke*, and the *League* which hee tooke at[85] *Anlaf*, and others (the *Captaines* of the *Danish Armie*) is intituled to be made *by him and all his* wise-men.(†) And certaine other *Articles* [*256] there be, though hitherto not imprinted, of a *Parliament* that was assembled in the yeere after *Christ*, 1008. which fell under the Reigne of the same King, which are there reported to have passed under the *authoritie* of the King, and his *Wise-men*, both *Spirituall* and *Lay*,[86] in which said last ordinances, this one thing for this purpose, is worthy the observation. That whereas in the beginning of the *Lawes*, all the *Acts* are said[87] to passe from the King, and his *Wise-men* both of the *Clergie* and *Laitie*; in all the *body* and *processe* of the *Law* each *Statute* saith thus, *And it is the advice* of our Lord, and his *Wise men*. So as it seemeth plainly that it was then[88] a received forme of speech, to signifie both the *Spiritualty* and *Laitie* (that is to say) the *Nobilitie* and *Commons* by the onely word *Witena*, or *Wise-men*.

[*257] Finally, those *Lawes* of the great *King*, and *Monarch*, *Canute*, or *Knowt*, which he made at *Winchester*, and be yet remaining, doe beare *face*, and *testimonie*, that they were made by *him*, and his *Wise-men*.(‡)

And there is an ancient written Treatise (entituled, *Modus tenendi Parliamentum tempore Regis Edwardi filii Ethelredi*) to be seene in many hands, purporting the very *order*, *forme*,

(†) *Ealles angelcynnes wittan, Foedus Alrudi.*
(‡) *Mid his witena getheaht gered.*

---

[85] tooke at] *F*; strock with *H BT*.
[86] Spirituall and Lay] *F BT*; *om.* *H*.
[87] said] *F*; layd *H BT*.
[88] then] *BT*; *om. F H*.

and *manner* of all this stately *Court*, and *solemne Assemblie*.

Now as these written *authorities*, do undoubtedly confirme our *assertion* of this *continuance* of this manner of *Parliament:* So is there also unwritten *Law*, or *Prescription*, that doth no lesse infallibly uphold the same.

For it is well knowne, that in every quarter of the Realme, a great many of *Burroughs* doe yet send *Burgesses* to the *Parliament*, which [*258] is neverthelesse so ancient,[89] and so long since decayed, and gone to nought, that it cannot be shewed that they have bin of any *reputation*, at any time since the *Conquest*, and much lesse that they have obtained the *priviledge*, by the Grant of any King succeeding the same: So that the *interest* which they have in *Parliament*, groweth by an ancient usage before the *Conquest*, whereof they cannot shew any beginning; which thing is also confirmed by a contrary usage in the selfe-same thing; for it is likewise knowne, that they of ancient *Demeasne* doe prescribe, in not sending to the *Parliament;* for which reason also, they are neither *Contributers* to the *Wages* of the *Knights* there, neither are they bound by sundrie *Acts* of *Parliament*, though the same be generally penned, and doe make no exception of them.

[*259] But there is no *ancient Demeasne*, (saving that onely which is described in the *Booke* of *Doomes-day*, under the *Title* of *Terra Regis*) which of *necessitie* must be such, as eyther was in the *hands* of the *Conquerour* himselfe, who made the *Booke*, or of *Edward* the *Confessor*, that was before him.

And so againe, if they of *ancient Demeasnes*,[90] have ever since the *Conquest*, prescribed not to send *Burgesses* to the *Parliament;* then (no doubt) there was a *Parliament* before the *Conquest*,[91] to the which they of *other places* did send

[89] is neverthelesse so ancient] *F;* neverthelesse be soe so ancyently *H BT.*

[90] Demeasnes] *F;* Demeasne *H BT.*

[91] the Conquest] *F BT; om. H.*

their *Burgesses:* Which seeing it is so, let us come yet neerer, and *examine*, whether the same *Order* hath also beene continued ever since that time, or no.

[*260] The[92] continuance of the Parliament after the Conquest.[92]

To looke for a *Parliament* assembled of the *English Nobilitie*, and *Commons*, soone after the *Conquest*, were but to *labour*, without expectation of *good speed;* for, *Silent Leges inter arma:* And during all the reigne of the *Conquerour*, eyther the *Sword* was not put up into the *Scabbard;* or, if it were, the *Hand* was alwayes upon the *Hilt*, readie to draw it:[93] So unwilling, on the one part, were the *Englishmen* to beare the *Yoake*, that rather their *Obedience* was to bee *compelled*, than their *Opinions* to bee *consulted:* and so haughtie, on the other part, were the *Norman Victorers*, that to bee called an *Englishman*, was, in their eye, a great *contumelie*, and *reproach*.

[*261] His Sonne *William* also, did rather pretend in *words* some release of the former *austeritie* in *Government*, than performe it in *deed*, and *experience:* But his other Sonne (the first *Henry* that ever reigned here) did not onely at his *Coronation* promise *restitution* of St. *Edwards Lawes*, as wee call them; but also delivered out his free *Charter* of the *Grant* of the same: in which, as *Matthew Paris* reporteth, hee acknowledgeth, that hee was *Crowned* by the *Common Councell* of the *Barons* of the *Realme* of *England*.

And here it may happily seeme strange to affirme, that this was a full *Parliament*, in which there is no other mention, but of the *Barons* onely. But if it bee considered; first, That the *Germans* expound, and render the word *Baro*, by *Freihers*, a *Free-man;* then, that *Matthew Paris* saith, That the Citizens

---

[92] The . . . Conquest] *F BT; om. H.*

[93] draw it] *F;* drawe againe *H;* drawe it againe *BT*.

[*262] of *London* were at that time called *Barons;* and also, that even yet both the *Burgesses* of the *five Ports* doe passe under the same *Name*, and that everie man (almost) hath his *Court Baron:* It shall not altogether bee without ground, to say, that both the *Nobilitie* and *Comminaltie* of the *Realme* were meant under these words, *The Barons of the Realme;* the rather, because that speech is accompanied with the words, *Common Councell;* by the which, all our ancient *Writs*, that bee grounded upon old *Statutes*, doe signifie the *Parliament:* And for that also, the selfe-same *Authour* doth afterwards use the words, *Communis assensus Baronagii*, when he intendeth to signifie a just Parliament.

Howbeit, since I labour not with any penurie of *proofe*, I will relinquish the advantage of this matter; [*263] desiring onely that[94] may bee called to memory, which *Polidore Virgil* hath before acknowledged, concerning the restitution of the forme of *Parliament*, made by the same King, of whom also the *Saxon Chronicles* of *Peterborough Abbey* doe testifie, That in the yeere after *Christ*, 1123. he sent his *Writs* over all *England*, and bad his *Bishops*, *Abbots*, and all his *Theins* (which signifieth as much as *Baron* before) that they should come to his *Wytena Gemote* on *Candlemas* day at *Glocester*.

But to leave him, and to leape over *Stephen* (because hee strived longer for the *Crowne*, than hee enjoyed it) King *Henry* 2. saith *Mathew Paris*, in the yeere of our *Lord Christ*, 1185. *Convocavit Clerum Regni, & populum cum omni Nobilitate apud fontem Clericorum.*(†)

And yet againe, to passe over his [*264] sonne *Richard*, that spent the most part of his Reigne in *battell* abroad; and to come to his sonne *Iohn*, that passed a great part of his time in *Civill Warres* at home; you may finde in the *Tower*, *Inter*

(†) *Clarkenwell.*

---

[94] that] *F;* that that *H BT.*

Volumina Recordorum Cancellariae de Patentibus Anno 6. Regis Iohannis in dorso, this *Writ; Rex, &c. Vic. Rotland, &c. Sciatis quod provisum est cum assensu Archiepiscoporum, Comitum, Baronum, & omnium fidelium nostrorum Angliae, quod novem milites per totam Angliam inveniant decimum militem bene paratum equis & armis, ad defensionem Regni nostri, & quod illi novem milites invenient decimo militi quolibet die duos solidos ad liberationem suam, &c.*

I read moreover in the same *Mathew Paris*, That King *Henry* the 3. did, *Anno Dom.*[95] 1225. call together *Omnes Clericos, & Laicos totius Regni*, which *Assemblie* the same *Writer* [*265] in some places expresseth by the words *Universitas Regni.*

But what need I to hang long[96] upon the *credit* of *Historians*, seeing that from this time downeward the *Authenticke Records* of the *Parliaments* themselves doe offer me present helpe.

Magna[97] *Charta* Parliament, Charter in Parliament.[97]

The great *Charter* of *England*, which passed from this King about this time, and for which the *English men* had no lesse striven, than the *Trojans* for their *Helena;* beareth no shew of an *Act of Parliament:* and yet I will prove, by the depositions of two sundrie *Parliaments*, that it was made by the common consent[98] of all the Realme, in the time of K. *Henry* 3. for so saith the Statute, called, *Confirmatio Chartae, Anno* 25. *Edward* 1. in flat termes; and the *Statute* (†) made at *Westminster*,

(†) *Stat.* 15 *Ed.* 3. *cap.* 1. *Confirme les* 2. *Char. & auters Stat. ft. per le Roy, Peers, & Com.*

---

[95] Anno Dom.] *F;* in the yeare of our Lord god *H BT* (*BT omits the word* god).

[96] long] *F;* longer *H BT.*

[97] Magna . . . Parliament] *F; om. H BT.*

[98] consent] *F;* assent *H BT.*

Anno 15. *Edward* 3. *cap.* 1. saith, That it was made by the [*266] *King, Peeres,* and *Commons* of this *Land.*

In the 20. yeere of the same King *Henry*, the *Statute* of *Merton* was published, which saith thus; *Provisum fuit, & concessum tam a praedictis Archiepiscopis, Episcopis, Comitibus, Baronibus, quam ab ipso rege, & aliis.*

In the 25.[99] yeere of his reigne also was the *Statute* of *Marlebridge*, made *Providente* (as it selfe speaketh) *ipso domino rege ac convocatis discretioribus ejusdem Regni. Regni*[1] *tam majoribus quam minoribus provisum est Statutum, &c.*[2]

The *Statute* of *Westm.* the 1. which was made in the 3. yeere of K. *Ed.* 1. hath this *title:*

> The establishments of K. *Ed.* made by his *Councell*, and by the assent of his *Arch-Bishops, Bishops, Abbots, Priors, Earles, Barons,* and all the *Comminalty* of the *Land* thither summoned.

[*267] The *Statute* made at *Glocester* in the sixth yeere of the same Kings Reigne, is there said to be made thus; *Purvenant le Roy & appelles le plus discretes de son Royalme auxibien des grand res*[3] *come des meinders stabilie est, & concordantment ordonne.*

To draw to an end, King *Edw.* 2. held a *Parliament* in the 14. yeere of his reigne, wherein are these words, *Le Roy per assent des prelates, Contes, Barones, & touts*[4] *le comminalty de son Royalme, en le Parliament, &c.* And the like speech hath he in another *Statute* that hee made, *Ne quis occasionetur pro morte* Petri *de* Gavestone.

---

99 In the 25.] *F;* And in the 25. *H;* And in the 52. *BT.*

1 Regni. Regni] *F;* Regni *H BT.*

2 est Statutum, &c.] *F;* est, statutum etc. *H BT.*

3 grand res] greind res *F;* greinders *H BT.*

4 touts] tout *F H BT.*

I doe not think that I shall need to seeke for further *proofes* amongst the *Records* of *Parliaments* after this time; for they doe from henceforth not onely shew themselves in such *store* and *plenty*, but doe also set forth the severall *estates* themselves, [*268] the *duty* of their *presence*, the *paines* of their *default* or *departure*, and sundry other *circumstances* so particularly and plainely, as I might well be *charged* if I would stand upon them in a *matter* not *doubtfull*, to have used *speech* nothing needfull.

And yet lest any man should suspect, that any of the two lower *estates* of this *Assemblie*, derived his *voyce*[5] in *Parliament* from the *authoritie* of these latter *Lawes*, I must leave him to understand, that in one short *Statute* of *Parliament*, holden in the first yeere of K. *Richard* 2. *Statute* 2. *c.* 4. he may read it foure severall times plainely spoken, and[6] this was done anciently, and of old time. So that here againe also, *prescription* is ready to serve the *turne;* and to say the *truth*, this *one Law* may *stand* for an *interpreter* of all the rest: for whether they be said to be made by the King and his *Barons;* or by [*269] the *King*, and his *Clergie* and *Laitie;* or by the *King*, and his *Discreter*, men both great and small; or by the *common consent* or[7] *Councell* of the[8] *Realme*, as I have alreadie shewed; or by the *King*, and his *Wise men;* or by the *King*, and his *Councell;* or his *Common Councell;* or by the *King*, his[9] *Earles*, *Barons*, and other *Wise men;* or after such other like *phrases*, whereof you meet with many, in the *Volumes* of *Parliaments:* It commeth all to this one *point;* namely,

> That the *King*, his *Nobilitie*, and *Commons*, did ordaine and enact the same.

---

[5] voyce] *H BT;* maine voice *F.*
[6] and] *F;* that *H BT.*
[7] by the common consent or] *F H. BT; om. H.*
[8] the] *F;* all the *H BT.*
[9] King, his] *F BT;* King and his *H.*

And which is more, if you shall finde any *Acts*[10] of *Parliament*, seeming to passe under the *Name* and *Authoritie* of the *King* onely, as there be some that have that shew indeed; yet you must not by and by *judge*, that it was established without the *assent* of the other *Estates*.

[*270] To take one example for the rest: The *Statute* of *Gloucester*, made the 6. of *Edw*. 1. speaketh thus:

> Our Soveraigne Lord the King, for the amendment of the *Land*, hath provided these *Statutes*, under-written:[11]

But yet the *Statute* made at *Westminster*, the[12] 13. yeere of that King, *cap*. 18.[13] and the *Statute* of *Quo warranto*, set forth in the 30. yeare of the same King, also reciting that *Statute* of *Glocester*, doe plainely acknowledge the one;

> and[14] it was provided by the more discreet men of the *Realme*, as well of the high, as of the low degree, being called together; (and the other, that it was) made by the *King*, calling together the *Earles*, *Prelates*, *Barons*, and his *Councell*.

And therefore it is well noted by *Iudge Brooke; And*[15] *though* Magna Charta, *and sundrie other*[16] *old* Statutes, *doe run in the* Name *of the* Prince *onely, yet the* [*271] *other two*[17] Estates *are supplied, in all good understanding*.

Againe, whether the *forme* of an *Act* be thus:

> The *King*, with the *assent* of the *Lords* & *Commons*, establisheth; (or thus,) It is *enacted* by[18] the request of the *Lords* & *Commons*, whereto the *K. assenteth;* (or thus,) By the *assent* of the *King*, & of the *Lords Spirituall*

[10] Acts] *F;* Act *H BT.*
[11] under-written] *F;* under written etc. *H BT.*
[12] the] *F;* in the *H BT.*
[13] cap. 18.] *om. F H BT.*
[14] and] *F;* that *H BT.*
[15] And] *F;* that *H BT.*
[16] other] *F BT; om. H.*
[17] two] *F; om. H BT.*
[18] by] *F;* att *H BT.*

& *Temporall*, & of the *Commons*, it is *enacted;* (or thus,) It is *enacted* by the *authoritie* of this present *Parliament:*

It is also *one* in *effect*, & *substance;* for the words *assenteth* and *enacteth*, be *equivalent* in this *case*, as it is holden, 7. *H.* 7. 14. & 11. *H.* 7. 25. Whereas otherwise, the *necessitie* of the *assent* of all the three *Estates* in *Parliament* is such, as without any *one* of them, the *rest* doe but lose their labour. For that fell out upon a time, that the K. in *Parliament* willed, that a certaine man should be *attainted*, and should lose his *lands;* [*272] whereunto the Lords *assented:* But because there was nothing spoken of the *Commons* agreement,[19] it was adjudged by all the *Iustices*, 4. *H.* 7. 18. That this was no *Act* that might *binde;* and therefore the *partie* was *restored*.

Hitherto of the *continuance* and *consent* of this our *chiefe* and *highest Court;* whereunto, after I shall have added a word or twaine of the *Iurisdiction* thereof, I will make an end.

If all the[20] *Iudgements*, as *Cicero* said, be *conversant*, either in the *punishment* of *offences*, or in the *decision* of *Controversies;* then is the *judgement* of our *Parliament* of as ample *Authoritie*, as the *Sentence* of any, or all other *Courts* whatsoever; for it delivereth *Lawes*, that doe *binde* all *persons*, in all *causes*, as well *Ecclesiasticall*, [*273] as *Temporall*, whereof you may see a great many of[21] *examples* in the *volume* of the old *Saxons Parliaments;* how strange a thing soever our *Popish Clergie* of latter times have thought that to be.

It hath also *jurisdiction* in such *cases* which have need of *helpe*, and for which there is no *helpe* by any *Law*, already in *force;* And whereas the erronious *Iudgements* of any other *Courts*[22] must be *reversed* by a *higher authority;* this *Court* doth not onely *reverse* the *errors* of the *Kings Bench*, which is

---

19 agreement] *om. F H BT.*
20 the] *F; om. H BT.*
21 of] *F; om. H BT.*
22 any other Courts] any Courts *F;* anie other Courte *H BT.*

superiour to all the *other;* but it may also *amend* the *errors* committed in the *Parliament* it selfe, if any such shall at any time appeare.

Thus have I runne along our *Courts* of all *kindes*, and have said (as I was able) severally of these *Lay*, and mixed *Courts* of *Records*,[23] deriving them from the *Crowne*, [*274] their *originall*, and drawing them by one and one (as it were so many *Roses*) from the *Garland* of the *Prince;* leaving neverthelesse the *Garland* it self *undespoyled* of that her *Soveraign vertue*, in the *administration* of *Iustice:* or as *Bracton* saith well; *Rex habet ordinariam Iurisdictionem, & omnia jura in manu sua, quae nec ita Delegari possunt, quin ordinaria remaneant cum ipso rege.* And therefore whatsoever *power* is by him committed over unto *other men*, the same neverthelesse remaineth still in *himselfe*, in so much as he may take knowledge of all *Causes*, unlesse they bee *Felonie*, *Treason*, or such other;[24] wherein, because he is a *party*, hee cannot *personally*[25] sit in *judgement*, but must performe it by his *Delegates*.

And this *supreme jurisdiction* reserved (as I told you out of *Britton*) to the *King himselfe*, is either altogether [*275] *silent*, or else it speaketh at the *Board* of his *Privie Councell;* the which[26] is so *incorporate* to him, as that it is said to speake with his owne *mouth*,[26] and that but *rarely*,[27] for such *reason*, as you have seen before.

Now therefore, as *God* is highly to be thanked, that these *Flowers* of *Iustice* are thus *delivered forth*, and *Dispersed abroad:* So is *hee* also heartily to bee prayed unto, that those which *occupie* the *place* of *Iustice* by them, may so behave themselves as it may appeare, that they doe not *exercise* the *Iudgements* of *man*, but of *God himselfe*, the *chiefe Iustice*

---

[23] Records] *F;* Record *H BT.*
[24] other] others *F H BT.*
[25] personally] *H BT; om. F.*
[26] the which . . . mouth] *F H;* (the whiche . . . mouthe) *BT.*
[27] rarely] rarely also *F H;* rarely (as I suppose) *BT.*

of the *World;* for so shall the good be *succoured*, and the *evill suppressed*, so shall the *Iudges* themselves be well *acquitted*, so shall her *Majestie* be duely *served*, and *God himselfe* honoured aright.

[*276] *It had beene fit, I know, to have added hereunto, as an* Appendix, *the beginning of the* Houses of Law *commonly termed, for that they did flow out of the*[28] Courts, *the* Houses, *or* Innes of Court, *and also*[29] *to have annexed a* Catalogue, *or* Table *of the* names *of all the* Chancellours, Iustices, *and* Iudges *themselves: But because there is not, so farre as I can yet learne, any certaine* Monument *of the* one, *and for that it requireth a great*[30] search *of* Records, *whereunto I have no* accesse, *to performe the* other: *I must leave them both to such as can, and will better travaile in that* behalfe.

FINIS.

---

[28] the] *F;* these *H BT.*
[29] also] *H BT; om. F.*
[30] a great] *F;* great *H BT.*

Appendix

ARCHION,

OR,

A COMENTARY

UPON THE HIGH COURTS

OF

IVSTICE

IN ENGLAND.

Compiled by *William Lambard* of *Lincolns-Inne*, Gent.

LONDON:

Printed for *Daniel Frere*, and are to be ſold at his ſhop in little *Brittaine*, at the ſigne of the Red Bull, 1635.

Facsimile of the title page of Frere's edition

Appendix

The Problem of the Author's Text

INVESTIGATION of the text of the *Archeion*, as printed, faces first of all the fact that two different editions appeared in 1635, the only year of its publication. The Stationers' Register for that year gives the essential information. On March 27 a book called the *Archion* was entered against the name of Daniel Frere as printer. On July 1, however, this entry was cancelled and replaced by another, in the names of Master Seile and Daniel Frere, for the same book now called the *Archeion*, "being the true originall Copie from the Authors executor."[1] The title page of this second edition similarly announces it as "Newly Corrected, and enlarged according to the *Authors* Copie," and the following note to the reader is signed "T. L.," obviously Thomas Lambarde, the author's grandson and heir. It is this second and corrected edition that is reprinted in full above.

At first glance, Frere's unauthorized edition seems to deserve no further consideration. T. L.'s note to the reader calls attention to its many "crying errors," protesting, in fact, that "this late *aspersion*" on "so worthie an *Ancestor*" calls "upon me, to *vindicate* him from that *wrong* (if any such can be) and my selfe from an imputed *Apathie*." We do find errors impairing the sense on page after page of the Frere edition. Its renderings of words that William Lambarde had written in his favorite Saxon letters are striking instances: the Frere edition presents

---

[1] *A Transcript of the Registers of the Company of Stationers of London 1554–1640*, ed. Edward Arber (London, 1875–94), IV, 335 and 341.

us with "*Micel zemore perenazemore* and *Ealpapire nazmore*" for what under T. L.'s direction was more properly read as "*Micel-Gemot*, *Witena-Gemot*, & *Ealrawitena-Gemot*" (p. *243). Frere's errors may, of course, have been due to reliance on a faulty manuscript, but their character suggests that he himself was largely responsible. The gibberish just now quoted is nothing more than what an unintelligent printer might make of the correct Saxon letters. There can hardly have been any proof-reading of Frere's book, for the catchwords on two pages are in error,[2] and one omission is clearly that of a line of print (p. *156 above). It is unfortunate that since 1635 the Frere edition has been circulating as widely as the corrected edition has.[3] Indeed some scholars have used the former as if it were the only edition.

Not much seems known about the characters in this episode of 1635. Thomas Lambarde, according to the family diary, was nineteen years of age; the death of his father the preceding August had made him head of the family.[4] That event may have interrupted his schooling: he had entered Queen's College, Oxford, in November 1632, and he was being enrolled at Gray's Inn in London that same August 1634.[5] We have no further clues to his intellectual interests, except, to be sure, that he set his autograph in 1634 on a volume of the "Armes of all the Noble men" in Kent, perhaps presented to him on

---

[2] Frere edition, pp. 185, 235. Four years earlier there was a scandalously careless printing of the Bible which roused Archbishop Laud to comment, "I knew the tyme when greater care was had about printeing, . . . but now the paper is naught, the composers boyes, and the correctors unlearned"—*Reports of Cases in the Courts of Star Chamber and High Commission*, ed. S. R. Gardiner (Camden Society, N.S. XXXIX, London, 1886), p. 305.

[3] Thirteen copies of each have been noticed in American libraries—W. W. Bishop, *A Checklist of American Copies of "Short-Title Catalogue" Books*, 2nd ed. (Ann Arbor, 1950), p. 104, numbers 15143 and 15144.

[4] *Miscellanea Genealogica et Heraldica*, II (1876), 102 and 104.

[5] Joseph Foster, *Alumni Oxonienses (1500–1714)* (Oxford, 1891–92), p. 872. Thomas seems to have been admitted to Gray's Inn eight days

his succession to his father's responsibilities.[6] Daniel Frere, also, had entered on his career in 1634, by taking up his freedom in the Stationers' Company that July. His *Archion* appears on the Company's records as his first publishing venture, and the succeeding entry of July 1 surely amounted to a reprimand. Henry Seile, the Master Seile of that entry, was seventeen years his senior in the trade. Since the corrected *Archeion* was printed for Seile with no mention of Frere on its title page, the joint entry of July 1 seems to have amounted to a transfer of responsibility. Frere turned for the next few years to the publishing of much lighter works, and after June 1642 we find his name only a few times in the Stationers' Registers.[7]

A parallel incident occurred in 1641. William Hakewill, an experienced member of the House of Commons, had prepared some thirty years earlier a substantial treatise on legislative procedure, which thereafter circulated in many manuscript copies much as William Lambarde's various *Archeion* papers did in the same years. In 1641 someone printed Hakewill's treatise, as part of the flood of books and pamphlets let loose by developments in the Long Parliament. In July of that year we find Hakewill himself bringing out a second edition, explaining in its preface that the first edition, published without his knowledge, contained so many errors that he was obliged to produce one himself.[8] In this case, however, it was the author

---

after his father's death—Joseph Foster, *The Register of Admissions to Gray's Inn* (London, 1889), p. 205. This was presumably according to arrangements made earlier, and we find no evidence of his being subsequently at Gray's Inn. But his diary shows that in 1641 he moved his residence from St. Bride's parish, London, to the family home in East Greenwich—*Misc. Gen.*, II, 104.

6 Included in the sale of Lambarde family papers by Messrs. Hodgson & Co., June 18, 1924, lot no. 523.

7 *Stationers' Registers 1554–1640*, III, 684 and 687; V, xci. *A Transcript of the Registers of the Worshipful Company of Stationers from 1640–1708 A.D.* (London, 1913–14), I, 5–48, 164, 259, 295, 341.

8 Hakewill's edition, *The Manner How Statutes Are Enacted in Parliament*, was printed by order of the House of Commons' Committee for Examination of Bookes, July 7, 1641 —cf. *Stationers' Registers 1640–1708*,

who redressed the errors of an enterprising printer. In our case in 1635, William Lambarde had been dead these thirty-four years. We may wonder whether his young grandson had any special qualifications, as executor and editor, beyond family pride and an "Authors Copie" of the *Archeion.*

None of this would be of significance if we were not confronted with a few substantial differences between the Frere edition and the corrected edition, over and above the former's obvious errors of printing or copying. The character of these differences will be evident if we now summarize the contents of the two editions in a comparative table:

Frere's *Archion*		The corrected *Archeion*[9]
pp. A3–A3v	William Lambarde's letter of presentation to Sir Robert Cecil 1591.	pp. A3–A4v
pp. 1–28	General origins and classification of the courts.	pp. 1–23
pp. 28–54	Courts of Exchequer, Common Pleas, Admiralty, and Constable.	pp. 24–45

I, 29. In his short preface, Hakewill says, "Those my collections, I imparted many yeeres since to some of my friends (which being by the length of time multiplied into very many copies) one of them (and I thinke the falsest written of all the rest) was without my knowledge lately printed, and by the negligence of the Printer, the errors of the copie were much increased, insomuch that it pleased the honourable house of Commons, (because it concerned their orders) to take notice thereof, and take some order therein; by which I was induced to make this publication, being otherwise very unwilling to have appeared in print, and to have subjected myselfe to publique censure." On the following January 29 the House of Commons was moved at last to order "that the Printers do neither print or reprint any thing without the Name and Consent of the Author" —*Journals of the House of Commons*, II, 402.

[9] This is printed above, and the analytical table here may be compared with T. L.'s table of contents (pp. *A7–*A8v). This table here may facilitate locating, in the text above, any past reference to the *Archeion* that proves in fact to have been to the Frere edition.

pp. 54–72	Court of Chancery.	pp. 45–59
omits	(on the Chancellor's authority).	pp. 59–65
pp. 72–88	continuation, chiefly on the necessity, use, and abuse of Equity.	pp. 65–77
pp. 88–90	Court of Star Chamber: introduction.	pp. 78–79
pp. 90–109	1. Criminal offences requiring extraordinary help.	pp. 79–95
pp. 109–175	2. The King or Council as judge.	pp. 95–147
pp. 175–217	3. The Star Chamber the usual court.	pp. 148–181
omits	Offences specified by Statutes.	pp. 182–223
p. 217	Concluding sentence.	pp. 223–224
pp. 217–222	Warden's Court.	pp. 234–237
pp. 222–224	Duchy Court of Lancaster.	pp. 231–233
pp. 224–231	Court of Requests.	pp. 224–230
pp. 231–232	Presidents and Councils (of the Marches).	p. 231
pp. 232–233	Courts of Wards, Augmentations, etc.	pp. 233–234
pp. 233–277	Parliament.	pp. 238–273
pp. 277–280	Concluding paragraphs.	pp. 273–276

Both editions, it will be observed, purport to give us the text of the *Archeion* which William Lambarde presented to Cecil in 1591. But three major differences are apparent. In correcting the Frere edition from his "Authors Copie," Thomas Lambarde added six pages on the Chancellor's authority, then added forty-one pages on the statutory offences of Star Chamber, and finally changed the order between that and the section on Parliament to run instead: Requests, Marches, Lancaster, Wards etc., and Warden's. How can these differences represent simply mistakes by Frere?

We may find useful evidence in the manuscripts of William

Lambarde's book, which supplied the place of any printed edition up to 1635. As has been recently remarked in a catalogue, "MSS. of this work seem to be fairly common; they all differ considerably from the published work (edited by the Author's Grandson, 1635)."[10] But not quite all. Although as yet none has been located that agrees with Frere's text, we have one manuscript that is very nearly in agreement with the text as corrected by Thomas Lambarde. This is Harvard Law MS. 68, a small book (12mo) in a hand of about 1600, whose faithfulness is well indicated by the not unsuccessful attempt at the end to reproduce William Lambarde's preferred signature in Saxon letters.[11] This manuscript, when compared closely with the Frere and T. L. editions, proves to agree with the latter at all but some minor points, with the one major exception that it lacks the forty-one page section on the statutory offences of Star Chamber. This raises the question whether the section on offences does properly belong in the correct text which Thomas Lambarde was trying to produce. To simplify our procedure let us put this one question aside, without prejudging it, until we have examined the other parts of our problem.

Other manuscripts of the *Archeion* cast immediate light on the change of order between the T. L. edition and the Frere edition. All these manuscripts, so far reported or actually examined, contain simply one part or another of the final *Archeion*, in various stages of revision. In presenting his book to Cecil in 1591, William Lambarde called it his "Commentaries," in the plural, "whereof, some I penned sundrie yeeres sithence, others not long agoe, and the rest so lately, that your

---

[10] Messrs. Sotheby & Co., May 8, 1944, p. 28.

[11] Seymour de Ricci, *Census of Medieval and Renaissance Manuscripts in the United States and Canada* (New York, 1935–40), I, 1036. The page of this MS. that serves as its title-page has a rough table of contents agreeing rather with the Frere edition than with what follows in the MS. itself.

Honour may, if it please you, take the first view and reading of them" (p. *A4 above). Examination of the manuscripts themselves confirms this in detail. Now the whole class of shorter *Archeion* manuscripts containing the sections on the minor courts—the courts falling between Star Chamber and Parliament in the table above—shows just the same order as in the Frere edition. In this particular, then, Daniel Frere's edition evidently represents the original version of 1591. The corrected edition, which is supported by the Harvard MS., must represent a subsequent version.

Although an adequate report on these partial *Archeion* manuscripts must wait on the results of further study, it is possible for us to anticipate these results and indicate more specifically the relation of the earlier versions to our three full texts. For, by good fortune, two authoritative manuscripts written before 1591 are available: one is dated 1579, the other 1589, and both seem clearly to have been prepared either by or for William Lambarde himself. The first is Bodleian Tanner MS. 435, which consists of most of the 1591 *Archeion*, aside from the half of this that is devoted to Star Chamber; the other, Folger MS. 511121.1 at Washington (D. C.), is Lambarde's own copy of his treatise on Star Chamber, in the form in which this was copied off into the 1591 *Archeion*.[12] Taken

[12] The two MSS. have been studied in microfilm and will receive fuller attention in the report that Mr. Ward is preparing on the earlier versions of the *Archeion* commentaries. The Folger MS., purchased in 1952, was previously known only from Messrs. Hodgson & Co.'s catalogue of their sale, June 18, 1924, of the Lambarde family papers, in lot 507: "Of the Courte called the Starre Chamber, a 16th century Manuscript, on 52 ll., *with notes in the margin in Lambarde's hand, and his autograph on title, dated 1589.*" Personal inspection in the Folger Library confirms this description; the text in part, and the marginal notes and interlinear changes for the rest, together show virtually all the several modifications that distinguish the Star Chamber treatise as it appears in the *Archeion* of the 1590's from the largely identical separate treatise (presumably also of 1589) of which several copies are extant. Working from these other copies the present writer in 1952 com-

together, they provide a firm basis for distinguishing between earlier and later readings in our three main texts. It will be convenient from here on to refer to all these more briefly as follows: *F* (the Frere edition), *T* (the edition corrected by T. L.), *H* (Harvard Law MS. 68), *BT* (Bodleian Tanner MS. 435), and *WF* (Washington, Folger MS. 511121.1).

We have already noticed that *F* shows the original order of the courts, that found in *BT*, in its pages corresponding otherwise to *T* pp. *224–237. The next of our three major differences is the addition in *T* of six pages on the Chancellor's authority. In this respect, as also in a number of readings on the pages next following (*T* pp. *65–74), *F* agrees exactly with *BT*, Lambarde's earlier writing. The six pages must therefore have been written later than the version published by Frere—but when? Fortunately there is one clear indication within the six pages themselves, a mention of John Popham, Edmund Anderson, and William Peryam as currently heading the three courts of common law (*T* p. *64). This was the case for a number of years, but only after February 1593, when William Peryam became Chief Baron—even Popham's appointment as Chief Justice was only eight months before that.[13] It seems evident, therefore, that the version contained in Thomas Lambarde's "Authors Copie"—and also in *H*, which agrees with *T* here—was written after February 1593. The text which Daniel Frere published in *F* can alone represent what William Lambarde presented to Cecil in 1591.

But Lambarde himself had become a Master in Chancery in

---

pleted preparing for the printer the readings of the 1589 treatise and the argument presented here, before the Folger Library's fortunate purchase became known; it is gratifying that full study of the Folger MS. has led to hardly more than the changes corresponding to the modifications just mentioned, in substituting the authority of the Folger MS. for the less direct testimony of the other copies referred to.

[13] Edward Foss, *The Judges of England* (London, 1848–64), V, 411–412.

June 1592, and these six added pages on the Lord Chancellor, with the related changes made in the following pages on Chancery, deserve to be examined in the light of evidence recently collected on Lambarde's career after 1592 in Chancery.[14] As a common lawyer among men of the civil law, and as the Master assigned for the taking of oaths in the Alienations Office—where he was concurrently Lord Burghley's personal deputy for that office's administration—Lambarde may have been a minor figure in Chancery itself until May 1596. But in that month his good friend Thomas Egerton became Lord Keeper, and in the weeks and years that followed Lambarde seems to have been Egerton's chief assistant in Chancery. This position was hardly more than formalized in May 1597 when Egerton, who retained the position of Master of the Rolls, appointed Lambarde his deputy for the keeping of the rolls.

Most of the six pages with which we are now concerned, like many of the related minor alterations that follow, are devoted by Lambarde to a more judicious treatment of the difficult question when and how the Chancellor first obtained his independent jurisdiction. Within the six-page addition itself, once he had written out what he wished to add on this historical question, Lambarde continued for two more pages (pp. *63–65) to dwell on the preëminence of the Chancellor among the officials of the Prince—even though this particular passage seems rather out of place here, duplicating in considerable part what he had written earlier at the beginning of the preceding section (pp. *47–49). Only a little further on (pp. *73–74), we find the following revision: "In which behalfe this our Age hath greatly to thanke *God*, for that by the ministerie of our gracious *Queene Elizabeth*, hee doth not

---

[14] P. L. Ward, "William Lambarde's Collections on Chancery," *Harvard Library Bulletin*, VII (1953), 271–298.

onely leave unto us the right use of those *Courts* of meere *Law*,

but hath also hitherto placed in that *Pretoricall* Roome, or *Chancery*, men no lesse learned in the *Common Lawes* of this Realme, then accomplished with the skill of this *Moderation* of *Equity*." (*F* p. 83, and *BT*)

furnished with men of great learninge and integrity, but hath alsoe by her owne selection, placed in this *Praetoriall Seate* of *Chancery*, a man noe lesse deeply grounded in the learninge of the *Common lawe*, then thoroughly accomplished with the skill of this *moderacion* for *Equity*." (*H* pp. 56–57, and *T*)[15]

Only Egerton, surely, could have been praised in this fashion for his learning in the common law. And the deliberate change to the singular, "a man," could not have been made before May 1596, when on Lord Keeper Puckering's death Egerton became the sole figure in Chancery; until James I's accession he held both the Lord Keepership and the Mastership of the Rolls. Egerton was considered to owe his advancement in a special sense to Queen Elizabeth's "owne selection."[16] It seems certain that Lambarde made this revision after May 1596.

But to what extent are we safe in assuming that the revisions of this sort, the passages in which *T* and *H* differ from *F* and *BT*, all represent a single revision by Lambarde at some time after May 1596? Let us review them briefly. There are several minor ones early in the book. Lambarde, now for the first time, gives the Court of King's Bench a place by that name in his historical account, designating as King's Bench what he

---

[15] Cf. the variant readings given p. *73 above; the text of *H* is here preferred as more fully in keeping with the character of the revision.

[16] On Egerton and Puckering see *Dictionary of National Biography*.

had previously treated simply as the ancient court that followed the King (pp. *19, *33; cf. pp. *23, *29). Then in the section dividing up the lay courts of his day, he weakens his incidental condemnation of encroachments by King's Bench on the jurisdiction of Common Pleas (p. *22; cf. p. *23). Now other evidence has indicated that Lambarde earlier in the 1590's had argued vigorously against King's Bench's increasing use of the writ of *Latitat* for such encroachments; and a note written in 1608 tells us that injunctions granted by Chancery for staying such suits in King's Bench were common under Lord Keeper Puckering but *not* after Egerton succeeded him as Lord Keeper.[17] These minor changes exhibited in *T* and *H* certainly seem related, and seem to reflect Egerton's new policies in Chancery.

Next, within the same section classifying the courts, we find the words "limited" and "absolute" inserted to emphasize, for civil suits, the distinction between the courts of common law and the courts of conscience, the latter evidently being Chancery and Requests, then Exchequer Chancellor's and Marches (p. *22). This touch of emphasis is interesting, for the changed order of the courts further on in the book shows Requests and Marches brought forward to follow immediately after Chancery and Star Chamber, which represent the absolute power. And careful changes made in the last sentence of the classification section refer directly to this change of order (p. *23). In other words, minor changes in this one section show also a close interrelation with the major change that we noticed first, the change in the order of the courts.

What we find a few pages further on may be disregarded as simply an added scholarly parenthesis (p. *32; cf. also p. *236). But then comes the major addition on the Chancellor's

---

[17] *Calendar of State Papers, Domestic . . . Addenda, 1580-1625* (London, 1872), p. 506; Ward, "Lambarde's Collections," pp. 291-292.

authority, followed by a series of related editorial changes and climaxed by the sentence paying tribute to Egerton. Almost no further readings of this one class, where *T* and *H* differ from *F* and *BT*, are evident thereafter in the book. It does look as if Lambarde set about this particular task of revision simply to add to and strengthen what he had earlier written on the Chancellor and his court, and as if, in reading over the pages up to the point of major insertion, he made incidental corrections that reflect changes in attitude due to his new and more responsible position in Chancery after May 1596. On finishing the revisions on Chancery, he may have done little more than instruct his copyist to put certain of the courts later into what he now regarded as a more suitable order.

Is it, however, possible that *H*, Harvard Law MS. 68, in the several readings peculiar to itself testifies to further revisions made at the same time, revisions that the grandson did not incorporate in his corrected edition *T?* These readings are not such as to affect appreciably the general picture just now formed of the revision after May 1596, but their details may be of some significance. So we must record first that the text of *H* seems in its small details a relatively trustworthy one. Those of its peculiar readings that appear plainly to be errors are on the whole few, and with only a handful of exceptions (e.g., p. *95) are trifling changes of single words. Since in saying this we include as errors all not particularly meaningful deviations from *T* and *F* at points where either of these is supported by an earlier manuscript reading—and such readings are available throughout almost the whole book—this understates rather than overstates the faithfulness of *H*. What is even more solid evidence is that by rough count, out of the large number of variant readings in *H* differing from *T*, the number of those in exact agreement with the earlier authoritative text, *BT* or *WF*, is considerably greater than the number of all *H*'s other variants from *T*, only half of which can be considered as errors, even in the inclusive sense just indicated. This is the accumulated evidence of small details, many of them trifling, since in making up this count of about eight hundred variants each of the few substantial additions and omissions has been treated as a single variant.

But all this is probably just what we should expect. The title page of Thomas Lambarde's edition announces that it is "Newly Corrected," and Daniel Frere seems to have accompanied Master Seile to the Stationers' office to enter the new edition. It is not quite reasonable to suppose that Thomas Lambarde troubled to copy off any more than he had to from his handwritten "Authors Copie": his natural procedure would be to compare his copy of the Frere book with that "Copie," to note down the errors that needed correcting, and to arrange for the publication of the Frere edition thus corrected. We should expect therefore that many trivial deviations, and some not wholly trivial errors, would thus be carried over from the Frere edition's emphatically careless printing. The great majority of significant errors were in fact corrected.

So practically all of the readings, large and small, where *T* alters *F* prove to be ones in which *H* supports *T*; the few exceptions are significant and are to be discussed below. *H*, Harvard Law MS. 68, seems in short to represent faithfully the "Authors Copie" which Thomas Lambarde was using for his corrections. This is confirmed in particular by the fact that in no passage lacking in *H* (e.g., pp. *74-77) do we find *T* making any corrections or changes from the text in *F*. This notably holds true in the letter of presentation to Sir Robert Cecil 1591, if we may disregard two petty variations (p. *A4). The date which we have given to the version in the "Authors Copie" has made it rather unlikely anyway that this latter text of 1596 or later was prefaced by that letter of 1591.

We gather that Thomas Lambarde, while naturally convinced that his "Authors Copie" was more correct, was disposed to adhere to the Frere edition at such points as this prefatory letter—he evidently regarded the two texts as one and the same work. Even stronger evidence to the same effect is found in his failure to insert, in the Chancery passages right after the sentence referring to Egerton, the clause in *H* expressing satisfaction that in this day bishops were no longer made Chancellors, being "men meeter for Churches then for Courts" (p. *74). This clause, in almost exactly the same words as in *H*, is found in *BT* and the other copies of that early part of the *Archeion*. Its reappearance in *H* is evidence that William Lambarde did not omit it in 1591 or after May 1596. Thus it had evidently been omitted in the printing of *F*—and Thomas Lambarde simply did not reinstate it.

All this creates a strong presumption that where *H* provides an intelligible reading not duplicated either in Thomas Lambarde's text, or in *F* or the earlier manuscripts, such a reading nonetheless represents a further revision made by William Lambarde after May 1596. Such readings, to be sure, are few. The longest is the omission by *H* of the two suggestions for reforms in Chancery procedure (pp. *74–77). It seems probable enough from the circumstances that in his revision Lambarde deliberately omitted these paragraphs. Immediately after becoming Lord Keeper in May 1596, Egerton introduced a series of reforms, and Lambarde had an important share in putting them into execution. His own Chancery collection indicates that he laid before Egerton, in a more developed form, the first of the suggestions made here, while the second suggestion seems a matter that Egerton, with his experience in and respect for the common law, would have attended to promptly.[18] The inappropriateness of repeating

[18] Ward, "Lambarde's Collections," p. 291, cf. pp. 285-286.

these suggestions under the new circumstances must naturally have escaped the grandson, who found himself, indeed, confronted with the short and perhaps impolitic condemnation of Bishops as Judges in his "Authors Copie" (according to *H*), and the long and interesting pair of suggestions on Chancery reform in *F*, at one and the same point in his texts. It is understandable that Thomas Lambarde chose to retain the latter on passing over the former.

A short two sentences earlier *H* has an interesting insertion expressing firmly how serious it would be if the Chancellor failed to keep his jurisdiction within bounds—it might be "more sufferable and Convenient to have noe Courte of Equitie att all" (p. *73). The substance of this remark seems typical of Lambarde's attitude toward the competition between courts for jurisdiction, as expressed most fully in his passage on "The true moderation of Iurisdiction absolute" (p. *120); the new strength of language was not inappropriate now that Lambarde occupied a position of influence and responsibility in Chancery under Egerton. But this same forthrightness may have struck his grandson as somewhat out of keeping with the more modest tone of the rest of the *Archeion*, for the evidence is that he chose not to add it to the Frere text.

These two additional features of the revision of about 1597 occur within the series of editorial changes made by Lambarde in his section on the Chancery, following his six-page insertion there. At least one other change seems, on the same basis, to have been made by him further on in the book. The unexpectedly full survey of past clerks in the Star Chamber—there is only one slight parallel to this in all the treatments of other courts (p. *229)—has in *H* been much abbreviated at its close (pp. *162–163). The fuller form of this passage, which Thomas Lambarde evidently retained without change from the Frere edition, is also found in earlier manuscripts. More specifically, it is found in the final version (like *WF*) of

William Lambarde's commentary on Star Chamber, although not in the first version of 1586 which appears in such manuscripts as B.M. Add. MS. 24,926. In preparing the final version, Lambarde recast and greatly expanded what he had previously written on Star Chamber, and the sentences conspicuously abbreviated in *H* represented his payment of gratitude—Lambarde's words are explicit on this—to the man who had opened the way for him to the needed records: William Mill, the Clerk of the Council in the Star Chamber.[19]

This final version of the Star Chamber commentary was copied off, with the few additions and modifications that distinguish *WF* itself, to become the central section and largest part of the book of 1591. Hence the sentences of appreciation to "*William Mills*, mine ancient favourer" have survived in the printed *Archeion*. But we can well believe that William Lambarde himself deliberately left them out in his revision of 1596 or later, as *H* would indicate. The relationship between the two men had almost certainly changed in the intervening years. Lambarde had acquired high standing in another court, and Mill, we learn, had run into serious trouble in 1590 with the attorneys of his own court, who charged him with exacting exorbitant fees. Mill was, in fact, imprisoned for a short time in 1594, and by July 1597 Egerton had finally decided to restrain his fees, to the great distress of the Clerk.[20] Here again, the evidence of *H* seems firmly supported by the circumstances.

One more reading casts similar light on the reliability of *H*. Toward the end of the book (*T*), at the opening of the brief treatment of the Duchy Court of Lancaster (p. *231), we come upon an awkward two words. Mention is made of "the

---

[19] C. L. Scofield, *A Study of the Court of Star Chamber* (Chicago, 1900), p. 82.

[20] Scofield, pp. 64–67; James Spedding, *Letters and Life of Francis Bacon* (London, 1862–74), II, 56 n. 5, and 57.

same King *Ed.* 3," even though Edward III has not been referred to in the preceding pages. This might seem to be just another of Frere's minor errors, not corrected by Thomas Lambarde, for *H* and *BT* agree in omitting the meaningless words "the same." But it is in these pages that the author in his revision after May 1596 altered the order of several sections, and the earlier order, shown in *F*, had placed just before this the section on the Warden's Court. Looking at the last sentences of this latter section (p. *236), we find that (in *F*) Edward III is mentioned as the king under whom the Warden's Court probably took form—although, as *T* and *H* agree in showing, William Lambarde in his revision after May 1596 was able to insert evidence from the Issue Rolls that there was a Warden of the Marches even earlier, under Edward II. Moreover, this whole section on the Warden's Court was one of the few that do not appear in *BT* and so apparently were newly composed in 1591. In short, it was logically appropriate first to add the words "the same" in the text of 1591, as *F* indicates, and then to delete them in the revision after May 1596, as *H* indicates. Thomas Lambarde, while correcting the order of these sections according to his "Authors Copie," evidently failed to notice this accompanying editorial change.

We see from this that William Lambarde, revising his book after May 1596 to strengthen its passages on Chancery, did look with some care at later parts of it. This makes it more striking that he did not bring the book as a whole up to date. He not only left unchanged his final excuse that he had no access to the records (p. *276), but he also seems to have made no attempt to take account of the advances of scholarship among his acquaintances during the intervening years.[21]

---

[21] On the society of antiquaries from 1586 on, see Linda Van Norden, "Sir Henry Spelman on the Chronology of the Elizabethan College of Antiquaries," *Huntington Library Quarterly*, XIII (1950), 146–

It has seemed necessary to proceed with some care through all this evidence, for we have been holding at arm's length all the while a serious difficulty: the fact that Thomas Lambarde's edition includes the long section on the statutory offences of Star Chamber, which the Frere edition and the Harvard manuscript both lack. If we had begun our reconstruction with this fact, we should have supposed that the "Authors Copie" as reported in *T* was closer to William Lambarde's original writing than either the Frere edition or the Harvard manuscript. To put it more concisely, in this one respect *T* agrees exactly with *WF*, and substantially with the 1586 treatise on Star Chamber, while *F* and *H* agree exactly on the omission, as if representing a single later version. There seem to be no variant readings on these pages to cast light on the matter. When Lambarde revised his first paper of 1586 on Star Chamber, he turned the section in it on the statutory offences into something rather like an appendix, at the end of the *WF* version, so that no editorial changes were called for thereafter when it was added to or dropped out of the larger *Archeion*. The most that we can say is that, as an appendix, this section takes its place somewhat more awkwardly in the midst of the *Archeion* than at the end of *WF*. This awkwardness may possibly explain why Thomas Lambarde's edition, after restoring the marginal heading, "The double Authoritie of the *Star-chamber*" (on p. *174), for a passage that recalls the subject of the statutes, misplaces this heading in the table of contents so that it there comes as immediate introduction to the section on offences (p. *A8).

But the evidence that we have already assembled seems

152, 158. At least two works by other men were relevant: Richard Crompton, *L'Authoritie et Iurisdiction des Courts* (London, 1594), and William West, *Treatise of Equitie, the Iurisdiction and Proceedinges of the High Court of Chauncerie*, in his *Three Treatises of the Second Part of Symbolaeographie* (London, 1594).

rather too solid to be shaken by one contrary bit of evidence. Everything else points to the trustworthiness of *H* as a copy of the revision of 1596 or later, and several details have shown that Thomas Lambarde felt free on occasion to disregard his "Authors Copie" according to his best judgment. He could quite possibly have added the section on offences himself, taking it from the author's copy of the separate treatise on Star Chamber, our *WF*, that almost certainly lay before him among his grandfather's papers. It only remains for us to make sure that we have done full justice to the care shown by young Thomas Lambarde—or his associate also, if he turned to anyone else for assistance—in preparing for the printer his corrected text of his grandfather's book.

It should be remarked that Thomas Lambarde was presumably confronted with many jottings or marginal notes by his grandfather in the "Authors Copie"—as in other of William Lambarde's books—and could also see that this copy on which he was relying was not in the author's own hand. This last seems almost certain, for there is direct evidence that at least from 1587 on William Lambarde considered himself forced by his "decay of sight" to rely upon the frequently "foule workmanship" of copyists.[22] This is indeed the only possible explanation of a serious omission, in *F* and *H* and *T* similarly, of a line or two in Britton's enumeration of the thirteenth-century courts (p. *38), which produces nonsense by telescoping the Courts of Common Pleas and Exchequer and which is not found in the manuscripts of the original commentary (*BT*). There is a similar and equally serious omission in the second of the suggestions for Chancery reform (p. *76),

---

[22] V. B. Heltzel, "Sir Thomas Egerton and William Lambard," *Huntington Library Quarterly*, XI (1948), 202; Cecil Monro, *Acta Cancellariae* (London, 1847), p. 15. *WF* is clearly not in Lambarde's hand, and exhibits many errors corrected in the same hand and ink as his signature on the title.

but since we have seen reason for thinking that these suggestions were deleted in the revision after May 1596, this latter omission may alternatively have been an error in Frere's printing. It is the former omission that stands as clearest evidence that William Lambarde did not write out or even fully proofread his *Archeion* in 1591 or thereafter. Yet he cannot have considered the copyist whom he employed for the "Authors Copie" incapable of errors, and we have seen much evidence of his sharp eye for particular points that needed correcting. All in all, the grandson most probably had before his eyes in the "Authors Copie" both corrections by his grandfather and a few further minor errors by its writer, errors that did not appear in the Frere edition and that we may assume contributed to the number of such now found in *H*. These probably encouraged him to exercise his best judgment in his correcting.

The failure of Thomas Lambarde to correct in any way such omissions as the two just mentioned hardly reflects upon his diligence. Since the passage containing the second omission had no parallel in his own "Authors Copie" (according to *H*), he may not have read that one sentence closely. He can hardly have felt competent to judge the statements from the old lawbook called Britton: even if we suppose that he was reading law, he had been enrolled at Gray's Inn for only some ten months. At the start, in the first one-eighth of the book, he found more than two readings per page worthy of correction; his edition shows that many variant readings from *F*. Thereafter, as we might expect, he corrected less closely, except for one stretch of twenty-five pages much further on. It would appear, indeed, that his discovery halfway through his task that the Frere edition was fuller on William Mill—and agreed there with *WF*, which was at his elbow?—led him to feel rather less critical of *F*. But after three pages his corrections began again, and after ten more he was apparently convinced afresh of the need to adhere closely to his "Authors Copie" and so corrected as closely, for a space, as at the start of the book.

He evidently could not resist making a few editorial improvements, but only such as could not possibly alter the sense. A "for the advancement of," awkwardly balanced with a "for," was appropriately trimmed down (p. *26). In another place, *F* had plainly done an injury to the author's style by adding a second "very," to read "the very first Chapter of the very same Lawes"; the grandson in correcting this produced an editorial change by cutting out the wrong "very" (p. *250). These are fair samples of his own contributions to the text, those plain from the agreement of both *F* and *H* with the earlier manuscripts, as against his text *T* alone. Changes as small as these may alternatively, of course, have been due to the printer, but there is little other evidence to suggest that Henry Seile's men did not do a faithful job.

It would seem that Thomas Lambarde felt more free to emend and add to the marginal notations, including also the section headings, since prior to his printing these also appeared in the margins. But we cannot follow him clearly in this. Both *F* and *H* provide very few marginal notes apart from the main section headings,[23] and yet it is evident from such manuscripts as *BT* that Lambarde's own copies had notes more or less agreeing with those in *T*. Perhaps it was the grandson who decided, in one case, that in a section heading the word "moderation" would sound better than "mediocrity" for the chief virtue advocated by the book (p. *122). But items in the margin may have been particularly open to improvement by William Lambarde himself in his own book before or after *H* had been copied from it.

This particular possibility is, in fact, raised by six minor

---

[23] *H* even omits many of these, especially in the passages on Star Chamber.

readings in Thomas Lambarde's edition, and peculiar to it, that cannot easily be dismissed as editorial changes of the sort just now noticed. One is the insertion of the Latin text of the first words of King Ine's laws in 712 (p. *248); two others are the specifying of "*cap.* 20." and "*cap.* 18." in citing two different statutes (pp. *168, *270). There is little other evidence to suggest that the grandson was able and disposed to add such information,[24] and the three insertions are just the sort of thing that we find as marginal notes in *T*. The first has an exact parallel on the margin of another page (p. *251); and the next two are paralleled on an earlier margin by "*Cap.* 3. 4. *&* 5." opposite a mention of the *Articuli super Cartas* (p. *39). The assumption that these are William Lambarde's marginal notes is strengthened by the appearance of this last note in just the same fashion in his much earlier *BT*. It is probable, therefore, that Thomas Lambarde took the three from the margins of his "Authors Copie"—where the writer of *H* may have passed them by—and inserted them in his main text.

The three remaining insertions may seem even more trivial, but all occur within the short section on the Court of Requests. The first of them consists of the words "and his *Councell*" (p. *225) and follows so logically from the discussion of Star Chamber there referred to, that it may have been added as an editorial improvement at any moment of reconsideration—although Thomas Lambarde's editorial changes are elsewhere not as substantial as this. The next, an insertion of the words "noble *Persons*" (p. *228), will be briefly noticed later. The last simply substitutes the words "were wont to" for "doe" (p. *229), but it is supported by a change from "be" to "were" in a parallel statement (p. *224). This change of tense may be significant, for Lambarde, after all, was an historian.

[24] The insertion of "*cap.* 11." in place of "28. E. 1:" (p. *206) may possibly be contrary evidence, if Thomas Lambarde was copying that section directly from *WF*, as is suggested below.

The troubled history of the Court of Requests at any rate justifies our looking closely at the whole array of variant readings in Lambarde's paragraphs on this court. The section on this court (pp. *224–230) was apparently in 1591 one of the few written so lately that Cecil was offered "the first view and reading of them"; it is without significant parallel in *BT*, or indeed in any manuscripts of the earlier texts thus far examined. Conceivably Lambarde's detailed treatment of this court owed something to the fact that earlier in the same year, according to Sir Julius Caesar's memory, the Court of Requests had begun to come under attack from the common law courts. Caesar, the junior Master of Requests who became the chief figure in the controversy, was a great gatherer of records and current documents, and as the attacks grew in seriousness he set about assembling all the precedents he could find to justify the jurisdiction of his court. Part of these materials he set forth in a private printing of 1597. When in January 1598 he presented a more complete collection on the subject to Lord Burghley, he modestly suggested that if Burghley had not the leisure, "Mr William Lamberd, whoe is A gentleman of great learning & sincerity, or some other one or more of like sufficiency might be intreated to peruse suche Collections as I haue gathered."[25] These two prominent collectors of manuscripts probably were, indeed, known to each other before this. Several of the points made by Caesar in his argument read much like Lambarde's argument on Star Chamber in the *WF* version or the *Archeion*.[26] And Lambarde's close friend among the Masters of Requests, Ralph Rokeby, had died only as recently as June 1596.[27]

---

[25] *Select Cases in the Court of Requests*, ed. I. S. Leadam (Selden Society, XII; London, 1898), p. xxv; on the history of the controversy, see pp. xxiv, xxxvii, *et passim*.

[26] Leadam, p. xxvii.

[27] See the special entry in the Lambarde diary—*Misc. Gen.*, II, 101.

Let us then test our reconstruction by piecing together the various readings of *H*, whether or not also found in *T*, that should represent in this section parts of Lambarde's revision after May 1596. The new additions point out that the "*Masters* of *Requests* be sworne of the *Kings Councell*" (p. *224), that the King's Privy Seal "is yet still the originall *Writ* of this *Court*" (p. *225), and that the mode of appointment of the Masters is such as to "argue the immediate *authority* of the Prince to be exercised by them" (p. *229). Lambarde also suggests that the court has regular standing by calling the company of its Masters a "Bench" (p. *227). And two further insertions make a second statement about the Masters' oath more judicious but still strong: the Masters take the same oath "in effect" as the Councillors "of *estate*" (p. *229). These editorial changes of 1596 or later are virtually identical with the sense of Sir Julius Caesar's arguments at the time, and seem in generous support of them.[28] There was certainly occasion for this support. Stepney's case was now being carried before the common law courts, the case whose decision in Common Pleas in 1598 was afterwards celebrated by Sir Edward Coke as the decisive ruling that the Court of Requests was in reality "no Court that had power of judicature"—although the court seems in actual fact to have suffered no lasting injury thereby.[29]

It is worth noticing now that a letter of early July 1596 to Sir Robert Cecil, speaking of a vacancy in the Court of Requests, remarked that "Mr. Lambert, I hear, hath refused the

[28] We find it also added that the whole argument rests on "*Authorities*" as well as reasons (p. *225), which agrees with Caesar's insistence on the cogency of the precedents in his collections. Since we lack any earlier MS readings for this whole section, in *BT* or any equivalent, we cannot be sure that any minor variant of this sort was not simply a correction of an error by Frere, but they all fit our understanding of the situation remarkably well.

[29] Leadam, pp. xxxix, xlvii; Sir Edward Coke, *Fourth Part of the Institutes* (London, 1644), pp. 97–98.

offer."[30] For this bit of gossip reminds us that by this date Lambarde was at the height of his career, attaining a position of new responsibility and influence in Chancery. What now can we make of the three readings peculiar to *T*, the possible marginal corrections in the "Authors Copie" of the *Archeion*? The words "were wont to" apply to a key point in the controversy: the last of Lambarde's statements mentioned above is altered by them to read that the Masters—in past times only—"were wont to" take the same oath as the Councillors (p. *229).[31] A parallel statement earlier is similarly altered: the Masters "were," rather than "be," sworn of the Council (p. *224). This careful qualification of his support of Caesar is confirmed by strikingly similar evidence in Lambarde's own copy of Caesar's book of precedents. There, alongside Caesar's printing of "The oth giuen to the Kings Counsell Iudges of this Court" (21 Henry VII), we find the following marginal objection entered in Lambarde's hand: "This forme of Oathe is now altered . . . : and thereof ariseth the question about the Jurisdiction of this Court. For now (as it seemeth) they bee not sworne as Councillors."[32] It seems quite likely, therefore, that the few readings peculiar to *T* represent similar marginal or interlinear corrections by William Lambarde in his "Authors Copie."

What little we know of Lambarde's personal relation to Caesar and the Court of Requests has suggested that this change, from the generous "doe take the same *Oath* in effect"

---

[30] *Historical Manuscripts Commission: Calendar of the Manuscripts of the Most Hon. the Marquis of Salisbury*, VI (1895), 248.

[31] If we continue to trust such single variant readings, the words "in effect" were also cut out (p. *229), and the company of Masters was called a "Commission" rather than a "Bench" (p. *227).

[32] In Sir Julius Caesar, *The Ancient State, Authoritie, and Proceedings of the Court of Requests* (British Museum, shelfmark 1380. g. 21), p. 149. The words here omitted refer to Lambarde's handwritten copy, on the book's last leaf, of the current oath of the Masters.

to the careful "were wont to take the same *Oath*," was more than simply a correction of fact and involved a reconsideration of the whole question at issue. Possibly Lord Burghley early in 1598 did refer Caesar's ample collection of precedents to him—Lambarde was evidently still acting as Burghley's loyal deputy in the Alienations Office.[33] Or Lambarde may have become aware in some other way that he might be called upon for a careful opinion. Certainly he had Caesar's materials before him later in the year: his copy of Caesar's book carries at the head of its first page, in characteristically methodical style, the entry, "W. Lambarde: octob. 1598: of the guifte of D. Jul. Caesar, M^r^ of the Requestes." This gift by itself would sufficiently explain the one further insertion in *T*, the words "noble *Persons*" added to the listing of past complainants before the court (p. *228)—it would be quite in character for Lambarde to go with care through Caesar's collection of past records of the court and then insert this correction. All in all, it seems likely that it was during 1598 that William Lambarde was led to qualify his earlier endorsement of the contention that the Masters of the Requests were strictly members of the Council.

Perhaps, now, we have some warrant for dating the revision reproduced both in *T* and *H* as made within roughly the two years following May 1596, rather than later; for otherwise Lambarde's change of view on the court, probably occasioned by developments in 1598, would have produced changes in text rather than the corrections or marginal notes that seem to confront us in these readings peculiar to *T*.

This attempt of ours to visualize just how Thomas Lambarde proceeded as editor has uncovered some elements of

---

[33] Ward, "Lambarde's Collections," p. 274. Caesar made his suggestion on January 16, and Lord Burghley's death was on August 8.

special value in his edition, but it has not seemed to put in question any part of our previous reconstruction of the textual relationships. The validity of many of the above surmises can, to be sure, be put to decisive test only if Thomas Lambarde's "Authors Copie" itself is some day discovered to be still extant. But we have gone step by step through the possibly significant types and groups of variant readings, without finding anything to make it seem likely that *F* and *H*, even though omitting in identical fashion the section on Star Chamber offenses, stand together apart from T. L.'s "Authors Copie" and the author's *Archeion* of 1591. The testimony of the minor variants as a whole is equally clear and forceful: *F* and *H* are independent of each other.[34] Thus on all the evidence available, the section on the statutory offenses of Star Chamber can be supposed to have been a part of the author's *Archeion* only if it is also supposed that the agreement of *F* and *H*, in omitting it identically, was due to chance alone.

Is there anything, then, to suggest why Thomas Lambarde may have been led to add the section from another of his grandfather's papers, if this is what he did? The omission by both *F* and *T*—the two printings of 1635—of the passage in the manuscripts on Bishops as Judges (p. *74) is certainly suggestive. In 1635, at the height of Archbishop Laud's ascendancy, it was perhaps impolitic to print a quotable line of rejoicing that Bishops had been sent back where they belonged and not any longer "permitted to follow the factions of other

[34] Only three times, in the simple omissions of a "that" (p. *30) and a "then" (p. *256) and the insertion of a "not" (p. *115), have *F* and *H* been found to agree against *T* and *BT* or *WF*. Cases of agreement of *T* and *H* against agreement of *F* and *BT* or *WF* have been found 44 times, but according to our reconstruction all but two of these stand logically explained as revisions after May 1596. Cases of agreement of *T* and *F* against agreement of *H* and *BT* or *WF*, on the other hand, have been found more than 385 times. The three agreements first mentioned are thus much too few, as well as too slight, to be more than the products of chance.

men."[35] In 1630 Dr. Alexander Leighton had been severely punished for publishing a criticism of the clergy, and in 1634 William Prynne, haled before Laud and his colleagues for an offensive publication, had stubbornly compounded his offense by filing a cross-bill charging the bishops with usurping the King's prerogatives.[36] It was, indeed, the severity of the punishments meted out under Laud's direction in the Court of Star Chamber, in these very cases, that turned public opinion at just this time against the Court.[37] John Rushworth, in his documentary history published a generation later, comments on these trials by giving a respectful abstract of the strongest treatise in defense of the Court, and then simply remarking that "When once this Court began to swell big, and was delighted with Blood"—referring now explicitly to such matters as Prynne's twice-cropped ears—"then began the *English* Nation to lay to heart the slavish condition they were like to come unto, if this Court continued in its greatness."[38] It seems

---

[35] Only a few months later, March 1636, Laud was writing in his own diary, "*William Juxson* Lord Bishop of *London*, made Lord High Treasurer of *England*. No Church-Man had it since *H.* 7. time. I pray God bless him to carry it so, that the Church may have Honour, and the King and the State Service and Contentment by it."—William Laud, *History of the Troubles and Tryal* (London, 1694), p. 289, cf. p. 53. As Clarendon remarked later, this appointment "Inflam'd more men than were Angry before, and no doubt did not only sharpen the edge of Envy and Malice against the Arch-Bishop (who was the known Architect of this new Fabrick) but most unjustly Indisposed many towards the Church it self; which they look'd upon as the Gulph ready to swallow all the great Offices"—*History of the Rebellion* (Oxford, 1712), I, 99.

[36] F. S. Siebert, *Freedom of the Press in England 1476–1776* (Urbana, 1952), pp. 122–125.

[37] H. E. I. Phillips, "The Last Years of the Court of Star Chamber 1630–41," *Transactions of the Royal Historical Society*, 4th S., XXI (1939), 117–128.

[38] John Rushworth, *Historical Collections* (London, 1659–1701), II, 475. This is plainly the editor's concluding paragraph to the abstract he has given pp. 471–475 (apropos of "Mr. *Prynn*, . . . his losing his Ears the second time *Anno* 1637") of William Hudson's well-known treatise on the Court—*Collectanea Juridica* (London, 1792), II, 1–240 (the abstract is only of pp. 1–36, the rest of the treatise being more technical).

diction to the *Court* of the *Leet*, or of the *Burroughs* or *Tythings*, as it was then called.

The second and the *Hundred Court*, then named *Hundresmote*, was in those dayes appointed to bee holden once in a month at the least, and that was of like nature to the *Countie-Court*, (which is now kept once every moneth also:) And to the Court *Baron*, anciently called *Heal-gemot*, and corruptly *Haylemot*, that is, (as I said) the Court of the *Hall*, *Mannor*, or chiefe place which is now at this day to bee kept, and maintained once in three weekes, if the Lord will so have, and use it. Hundred Court. Court Baron.

I read further in the Lawes of the *Saxon* King *Edgar* thus, *Negesecenam man won Cyng rot &c.* Let no man seeke to the King in matter of variance, unlesse he cannot find right at home: but if that right be too heavie for him, then let him Sax. Lawes, Cap. 2. f. 79.

Facsimile of page 15 of Thomas Lambarde's edition

Ealpapire nazmore, that is to ſay, the *great meeting*, the *meeting* of the *wiſe men*, *or the meeting of all the wiſe men.*

For *Pirena* ſignifieth *Wiſe men*, *caſtua*, *all*, and *zemore*, *a meeting*; of which laſt word the names of *Shiremote* and *Folkemoote*, and *Halymoote*, (that is to ſay) the *Aſſembly*, or *Meeting* of the men of the *Shire*, of the men of a *Towne*, and of the *Tenants* of a *Hall*, or *Mannour*, had their beginnings alſo.

And as *Synoth* is more uſed in the Acts of *Parliaments* themſelves, ſo *Gemote* is more familiar to the Hiſtorians: Thus much aſwell of the preſent, as of the ancient uſuall name: now let us looke into the

Facsimile of page 240 of Frere's edition (see discussion in Appendix, p. 146)

likely that a young country gentleman, at that time, might have felt it wise to dignify further his own grandfather's outspoken defense of that Court. To add the long section on statutory offences from another of the family papers was to increase the weight of detailed scholarship associated with that defense—and also to bring out more clearly the quality of solid and judicious learning that properly attached to the name of William Lambarde.

On the pages above, Thomas Lambarde's edition has been reprinted with as little alteration as the present format will allow; items in the margins of that edition have been entered as subheadings to the left or as author's footnotes, according to their character. The variant readings of *F* and *H* are indicated in further footnotes.[39] There has been no intention of inserting such footnotes for any manifest errors, or for any evidently meaningless deviations from the readings of the earlier *BT* or *WF*, except such as amount to more than a word or two at a time. Many of the petty errors of *F* that Thomas Lambarde corrected have therefore been passed over. Similarly, no notice is taken of some of the petty errors that he evidently did not recognize and so allowed to appear in his own edition—although here the attempt has been to include any that may be of the slightest interest.[40] Next, since none of

---

[39] Correspondences of these with readings of *BT* and *WF* are regularly indicated. It has seemed proper to add a very few readings from these manuscripts that may indicate substantial errors in *T* not revealed by *F* or *H*. In quoting from the manuscripts all contractions (except in citations of statutes) have been expanded, and modern usage has been followed in substituting "v" for "u" (and vice versa), and "f" for "ff," to approximate the usage in *T*. In reproducing *T*, the long "s" has been modernized and quotations in black letter have been rendered as indented extracts, except in the case of a few scattered short phrases on pp. *249–256.

[40] An effort has been made to report all the few readings of *F* and *H* that may contradict the above reconstruction of textual relationships. Since the reconstruction raises the possibility that in the section on Star Chamber *T* is a direct copy of

our three main texts handles the author's Saxon and Greek words with any great competence, no variant readings are indicated for these, except in two cases at the start (p. *15), where the writer of *H* seems to have been rather more careful, and Thomas Lambarde rather less successful, than normally thereafter. Finally, there has seemed no need to give variant readings for what now appear as author's notes: these are lacking in *H*, and of all the citations of authorities in *T*'s margins, *F* shows only the last (p. *265). In spite of these exclusions the readings given represent a large proportion of the total noticed in examining the texts. It is hoped that they will contribute to a better understanding of the degree of care with which William Lambarde wrote, and also revised, his commentaries on the High Courts.[41]

WF, all of *WF*'s variant readings for this section that seem of any interest are given. Virtually in every one of these, *WF* is supported by the manuscripts of Lambarde's earlier texts on Star Chamber; and taken together they appear to show the same mixture of minor editorial changes and minor errors that we have seen as characteristic of Thomas Lambarde's work. Elsewhere all readings are given in which *T* stands alone against the other texts, since they appear to show not only Thomas Lambarde's own editing but also his grandfather's last corrections.

[41] Since the above was sent to the press, there has been an opportunity to examine manuscripts of the *Archeion* in English libraries. Nine manuscripts have been found containing the version presented by *F:* B. M. Harleian MS. 5206, B. M. Add. MS. 22,591, B. M. Add. MS. 48,055 (Yelverton 61), Lincoln's Inn MS. A. II. 3, Bodleian Carte MS. 174, Cambridge Trinity MSS. 1463 and 1474, and Northants MSS. Finch-Hatton 28 and 84. Three have been found containing the version presented by *H:* B. M. Lansdowne MS. 600, Bodleian Tanner MS. 288, and Northants MS. I.L. 3391. Inspection has revealed no divergence affecting the reconstruction presented above. The section in *T* on the statutory offenses of Star Chamber is lacking in all twelve manuscripts.

Bei Fragen zur Produktsicherheit wenden Sie sich bitte an:
If you have any questions regarding product safety,
please contact:

Walter de Gruyter GmbH
Genthiner Straße 13
10785 Berlin
productsafety@degruyterbrill.com